B-29 PHOTO COMBAT DIARY

THE SUPERFORTRESS IN WWII AND KOREA

CHESTER W. MARSHALL
WARREN THOMPSON

Published by:
Specialty Press Publishers and Wholesalers
11481 Kost Dam Road
North Branch, MN 55056
612/583-3239

Printed in the United States of America

Designed by Greg Compton

ISBN
0-933424-60-4

B-29 PHOTO COMBAT DIARY
TABLE OF CONTENTS

WORLD WAR II IN BLACK AND WHITE

There's an age old adage that proclaims the true evaluation of a picture. In essence, the message says: "A good picture is worth a thousand words!"

Thumb through a few pages of this *B-29 Photo Combat Diary* and we think you'll agree with the above adage! There are over 400 reasons to convince you.

Through pictures alone, with well researched captions of each, we are relating the story of the premier aircraft of World War II, the Boeing B-29 Superfortress, the people who flew them, and those who labored around the clock to "Keep 'em flying."

Having to overcome enormous obstacles, the B-29s, flying first from India and China, to reach Japanese targets, and eventually from bases in the Mariana Islands, were instrumental in bringing Japan to the surrender table *without an invasion of the Japanese home islands*. Air power of such strength demonstrated by the Twentieth Air Force's Superfortresses proved without doubt that for the first time in the annals of warfare a war was won without the necessity of defeating an enemy army in the field!

This is a fact of history—not a revisionist's proclamation of history!

The pictures in this volume tell the story about the men who made it all happen. There were the cooks and clerks, the armorers and the men from the Service Groups who toiled day and night to keep airplanes in the air.

And of course, there were the aircrews who manned the Superforts. Denny D. Pidhayny, Recording and Historical Secretary, 58th Wing Association, visualized the chores performed by the aircrews, and we quote: "To the aircrews, life went from a high pitch of combat flight to a lull of waiting. At times, life hung on thread and we saw the miracle of survival. There were wild stories that made truth stranger than fiction."

This first chapter, WORLD WAR II IN BLACK AND WHITE, portrays black and white photographs of the B-29s, crew pictures and different scenes and activity, the way of life in two Theatres of War, the China, Burma, India Theatre, where B-29 operations against Japanese targets began with the 58th Wing from bases in India and forward bases across the Himalayan Mountains in China, and the Pacific Theatre where two B-29 Wings, the 314th and the 315th were based; from Tinian, where the 313th Wing based, later joined by the 58th Wing from CBI, and the 509th Composite Group, the Atomic bombing group; and from Saipan the 73rd Wing, the first Wing to reach the Pacific and made the first B-29

strike against Tokyo, on November 24, 1945.

The second chapter, WORLD WAR II IN COLOR, portrays, contrary to belief of a lot of the people who were there, some of the finest full color pictures of B-29s and the people who serviced and flew the planes.

Chapter three, THE KOREAN WAR IN COLOR, portrays the same for activity by the B-29 Superfortresses in the Korean War. Since the Superfortress of the old 19th Bomb Group of WWII era were the first to go into

"She flies!" Those were the words Eddie Allen, chief experimental test pilot for Bowing Airplane Company, told the waiting crowd of co-workers at the end of a one hour fifteen minute flight of number one XB-29 at Boeing Field in Seattle, Washington. The date was September 21, 1942. Pictured is one of the first flights of #1 XB-29. The aircraft later called the B-29 Superfortress when production began, had a wingspan of 141 feet, was 99 feet long, was powered by four 3350 radial engines, each producing 2,200 horsepower, and was destined to become known as the principal airplane that won World War II. (ROBBINS)

WORLD WAR II

combat in the Korean War, these pictures will tell about the history of the airplane and its crews in that war.

And, finally, chapter four, THE KOREAN WAR IN BLACK AND WHITE, portrays the life and times and activity in the Korean War in rare black and white pictures.

We are indebted to many people who were so generous to loan us pictures from their collections for this volume. In all there are more than 400 pictures in this book. We are grateful to so many, but some few allowed us to use photographs from their collections that have never before been published.

People involved in testing #1 XB-29 named the aircraft *The Flying Guinea Pig*. Robert M. "Bob" Robbins was one of the early experimental test pilots under the leadership of Eddie Allen. Bob, pictured under the nose of #1 XB-29, was aboard the plane on 545 hours of the 576 total hours flown at the time it was scrapped on 11 May 1948. He was pilot-in-command for 496 of those hours. (ROBBINS)

Harry Changnon, Historian for the 40th Bomb Group, furnished us with most of the photos from the CBI Theatre, covering activity of the 58th Wing (XX Bomber Command) based in India and China and later in Tinian.

Ed Hering, with his rare pictures of the 509th Composite Group, and the 315th Wing at Guam, was generous in allowing us to take advantage of his expert photography, through the use of many of the pictures from his collection.

And there were many others, each recorded under the photograph they furnished for this volume. Like the authors of the book, every contributor is conscientious about the preservation of these pictures for this and future generations.

End of the road for *The Flying Guinea Pig*. Many hardships and heartaches took place during the experimental stages of the XB-29s between the first flight on September 21, 1942 and the trip to the scrap heap. On February 18, 1943, a

major disaster took place that almost put the testing project on hold. Flying #2 XB-29 Eddie Allen and some of his most experienced test monitors were killed in a crash caused by a fire in an engine that spread to the gas tanks in the wing . All aboard perished. (ROBBINS)

This graphic picture of the giant B-29 Superfortress was assembled by sections which were built separately. The world's most sophisticated bomber at the time, it was designed by Boeing Airplane Co. of Seattle, Washington. The Aircraft was larger and faster than another Boeing bomber, the B-17, and could carry a much heavier load much farther. (BOEING ARCHIVES)

WORLD WAR II

Built from scratch, the B-29 had many new innovations never before used by combat aircraft, including a remote-controlled firepower system, and pressurized positions for the eleven man crew located in three sections of the aircraft. This assembly line of B-29s are nearing the finish line at Boeing's giant new plant at Wichita, Kansas.

Production of the Superfortress, hampered by engine fires in the all new 3350 radial engines by Wright. By mid-1943 key personnel, many of them combat veterans, began arriving for new assignments to the newly organized 58th Bomb Wing in Kansas, to begin training in B-29s.

Capt Alex Zamry, Maj Robert Morgan, Lt L.Sorrentin

Early arrivals at Pratt, Kansas for training with the 40th Bomb Group were from left Captain Alex Zamry, Major Robert Morgan, and Lieutenant L. Sorrentin. They are shown in the 395th Squadron S-2I and Ready Room. Morgan was the pilot of the famous *Memphis Belle* B-17, who was among the first to complete 25 missions over German targets. He later joined the 73rd Wing and became a Squadron Commander in the 497th B-29 Bomb Group, and led the first B-29 raid against Tokyo November 24, 1944. (L. JONES/CHANGNON)

B-29 PHOTO COMBAT DIARY

Colonel Jake Harman, Commander of the 40th Bomb Group, checks his crew at the Chakulia Air Base in India. Colonel Harman landed the first B-29 to reach India in April, 1944. With him was Brig. General Blondie Saunders, who later pioneered the route over the Himalayan Mountains to the forward base of Kwanghan at Chengtu, China. (L. COIRA/CHANGNON)

Sleepy Time Gal was one of the early B-29 arrivals at the 40th Bomb Group Base at Chakulia, India. Brig. General K. B. Wolfe, 58th Wing Commander went to India long before combat crews arrived to scout out suitable sites for B-29 bases. He decided on building bases in the Ganges plains about 70 miles west of Calcutta. Bases were made ready at Kharagpur where both the 468th BG and the 20th Bomber Command were located. Other bases were at Chakulia, (40th BG); Piardoba (462nd BG); and Dudkhundi (444th BG). (L. COIRA)

Major Don Roberts and members of his crew check available maps of the area before the first B-29 strike against a Japanese target and Bangkok, Thailand of June 5, 1944. Brig. General Blondie Saunders, led the 112 B-29s on that first mission. (ROBERTS/DICKERSON)

WORLD WAR II

Major George Weschler's crew lines up for a picture while ground crew men standing at the nose of *Superstitious Aloysious*, prepare a cracked plastic window in the nose of the aircraft. James J. O'Keefe was Bombardier on the crew. The crew flew with the 25th Squadron, 40th BG. (SEETH/CHANGNON)

Lady Luck gets a new camel symbol painted on her nose which represents another "Hump Mission" from the 444th Bomb Group base at Dudhundi, India to a forward base in China, where fuel and bombs were stored until a supply was built up enough to fly a bombing mission against Japan or some distant Japanese target. Colonel Al Harvey was commander of the 444th Group. (DEARDORIL)

Dragon Lady arrived early in India to begin bombing and supply missions. As a mechanic stands by for a photo session, it is noted that the aircraft had finished two "Hump" supply hops and six bombing mission. (CHANGNON)

Beter 'N' Nutin nose art tells the story that this Superfortress was a real veteran of the 444th Bomb Group at Dudkhuni Airbase in India. Symbols painted on the nose indicate the plane had flown 18 bombing missions and 14 "Hump" supply missions. Regular B-29 combat planes had to fly bombs and extra

gasoline from Indian bases to forward bases in China, and stockpile enough supplies at the forward base to execute a bombing mission against Japanese targets. (A.O. EVANS)

Aircraft commander Jenstrom, center, standing, and crew, pose by the plane named for the noted Boeing test pilot Eddie Allen. Picture taken at Tinian in May, 1945. Charles Crecelius was a member of the crew. (CRECELIUS)

The Himalaya mountain chain, the world's tallest, lies between the B-29 bases in India and the Chengtu area where the four advance bases in China were located. This is one of the tallest mountain peaks. Heavily loaded Superfortresses were taxed to the limits to go over some of the peaks, and were forced to fly around them. (CHANGNON)

Each of the four Bomb Groups of the 58th Wing stationed in India had forward bases in China: The 40th BG at Hsinching, 444th BG at Dudkhundi, 462nd BG at Kiunglai, and the 468th at Pengshan. Before a major combat strike at Kyushu, in Japan or other targets in Asia, the 58th Wing had to transport bombs and supplies, including gas, to the forward bases before a raid could take place. *Himalaya Hussy* is shown flying over the rugged terrain. (CHANGNON)

Photographer gets ready to take a picture of *Lady Hamilton*, serial number 42-93828, which flew with the 468th Bomb Group, based at Kharagpur in India with a forward base at Pengshan in China. Later the *Lady* moved with the 58th Wing to West Field on Tinian Island. (A.O. EVANS)

These two B-29s were almost completely destroyed after a mission to Omura when they crashed at Ankang, China November 21, 1944. The plane nearest to the camera was #321 from 444th Bomb Group, and the other was #290 from the 40th Bomb Group. (N. WEMPLE)

B-29 PHOTO COMBAT DIARY

Assid Test must have just recently arrived at Colonel Carmichael's 462nd Bomb Group at Piardoba Air Base in India. No mission symbols appear on the nose, indicating no missions have been flown when picture was taken. (CHANGNON)

Gunners on *Sister Sue*, serial number 42-6342, of the 40th Bomb Group, are performing their chores before a mission by checking .50-caliber gun turrets, and loading the guns which are operated by remote control. (EVANS)

All precautions were taken at the forward B-29 bases in China. Camouflage was used extensively, such as this shown on a 40th Bomb Group aircraft, #306 at Heinching in September, 1944. The Japanese forces were a bit too close for comfort. (B. WOTPKE/CHANGNON)

Mechanics swarm over a Superfortress at a forward base in China. This picture was taken in 1944. Inspections were a daily routine because many of the gremlins caused problems in the early Superforts, especially the engines. (CHANGNON)

The Chinese people by the hundreds helped build the forward bases, mostly by man power alone, by breaking stones into small pebbles to building a foundation for the runways. Transporting gasoline in 55-gallon drums by primitive methods was another strange sight to the Americans. (OTTO KERSTNER)

Luckily, Chinese people were plentiful around the B-29 forward bases to do chores they were asked to do. Since there was very little modern equipment available to them, this primitive method is the way they transferred gas to be pumped into the Superfort's tanks. (CHANGNON)

B-29 PHOTO COMBAT DIARY

Fast Company looks ready to go as she sits in hardstand of the 468th Bomb Group. The fire extinguisher is out (near nose wheel), someone is finishing up inspection in the bombardier's area, and we can't explain what the folding cot is doing in the shade under the fuselage. (CHANGNON)

This picture was taken at A-1, code name for the Hsinching, China base for the 40th Bomb Group B-29s. The group of people are searching the skies for the 40th Group planes returning from a bombing mission against Japan. They are standing outside the control tower in early fall of 1944. (HARRY CHANGNON)

The veteran *Sky Scrapper* with unusual nose art sports six "Hump" supply missions while in India and a total of 39 missions, some of them flown from Tinian after the 58th Wing's Groups moved to the Mariana Island in the spring of 1945. *Scrapper* artist painted on the "Tiger saw-teeth" symbol used by the

Flying Tiger P-40s in the China operation earlier. (CHANGNON)

Devilish Snooks is about to get loaded up with 500-pound demolition bombs at Chakulia during March of 1945. In the background is the engineering building. Soon after this mission, *Snooks* and other B-29s of the 58th Wing loaded up and moved lock, stock and barrel to Tinian Island to join other B-29s Wings in the Mariana Islands for the final assault on the Japanese homeland. (CHANGNON)

Returning from a photo mission to Singapore on February 26, 1945, the Jim Lyons crew was forced to bail out after a Japanese fighter attack. Nine of the 12 men aboard were rescued from the ocean. Four, including airplane commander Lyons, pilot Mills Bale, Nav. Nathan Teplick and LG Louis Sandrick, were picked up by a British PBY aircraft. A British submarine, HMS *Seadog*, picked up four of the crew: Teplick, Lester, Dimock and Topolski. The bombardier, William Kintis, CFC gunner J.M. Moffit and tail gunner J.J. Carney were declared "killed in action." Their bodies were never discovered. (HARRY CHANGNON)

Bob Gaughan and crew pose by *Gone With The Wind* before the entire 58th Wing in India and China moved to West Field on Tinian Island for the final B-29 assault on the home islands of Japan. The move took place in the spring of 1945. Left to right, standing: George Larson, Jerome Freidman, Robert "Bob" Gaughan and Arthur Barry. Kneeling, left to right: Vernon Wilkening, Charles Benson, Irvin Smith, Thomas Payne and Ernest Hilyard. (HILYARD)

B-29 PHOTO COMBAT DIARY

The 73rd Bomb Wing with its four Groups, the 497, 498, 499 and 500 Bomb Groups, began arriving at Saipan, the first island in the Marianas group to be captured, in mid-October, 1944. Brig. General Haywood Hansell, commander of the XXI Bomber Command, with Major Catton and the crew, landed the first B-29 in the Marianas at Isley Field, Saipan, and began planning the beginning of operations against the Japanese homeland. The scene above from the air was to be one of the first sights seen by combat crews over Japan as they used cone-shaped Mount Fuji as the IP (initial point) on bomb runs to targets in Tokyo, about 60-70 miles away. (U.S. AIR FORCE COMBAT PHOTO)

With 16 bombing mission symbols painted on her nose and some very good nose art, *Lassie Too!* (with the 468 Bomb Group, stationed at Kharagpun, India) is ready for more action. (HARRY CHANGNON)

Army engineers, with their trucks and bulldozers, followed the assaulting Marine and Army troops onto Saipan which began June 15, 1944. They worked night and day to complete this airstrip for use by the B-29 Superforts. Seven days after the invasion of Saipan began, the engineers had filled over 600 holes and craters with crushed coral at the much bombarded Aslito Airdome (later named Isley Field), and had it in operation to land based P-47s. One strip of the airstrip was ready to receive the B-29s by early October. The 73rd Wing ground echelon preceeded the flight crew by a month or so to help build living quarters. (U.S. Air Force Combat Photo)

Above the clouds over Japan with two engines out. Engines number 3 & 4 have been feathered, and speed has been drastically reduced. The wing of another plane, right, indicates lowered flaps to reduce speed of that plane to remain with the damaged aircraft. The "buddy" system was effective because the accompanying plane could relay messages to a dumbo or a ship or submarine if the damaged plane had to ditch. Also, they could help fight off enemy fighters. Tail symbols were changed in early 1945 to one large letter for better identification. The T Square 8 became a big T, easily identifying that the plane was from the 498th Bomb Group on Saipan. Note the open door just after the white star. This means that the crew opened the door in this unpressurized section in order to throw out all excess equipment to lighten the load in the aircraft. (Ed Hering)

B-29 PHOTO COMBAT DIARY

Radio operator, William C. Taylor of Willard, MD., at his position on a Boeing B-29 Superfortress en route to Saipan in the Mariana Islands on November 6, 1944. (U.S. AIR FORCE PHOTO)

Double Exposure of the 3rd Photo Recon Squadron, based at Saipan early on and later moved to Guam, gets a thorough clean up job, all of which is duly recorded by a photographer hanging halfway out of the cockpit. Symbols indicate the airplane had been on 12 photo missions to targets in Japan. (JOHN MITCHELL)

A B-29B of the 331st Bomb Group, 315th Wing at Northwest Field, Guam, taxiing out for a mission against oil refineries in Japan. The B model is a modification of the A model. It has no gun turrets except the tail gun position. It also has a horizontal antenna, associated with the new radar system called the AN/APQ-7 "Eagle," a highly improved radar system. (ED HERING)

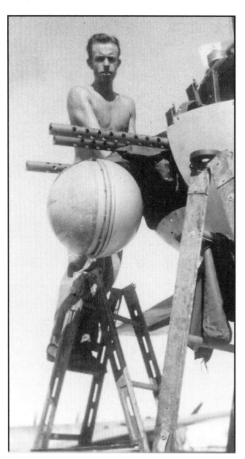

T/Sgt. Ed Hering, 501 Bomb Group, 315th Bomb Wing at Northwest Field on Guam, fights the heat without shirt (I think that's all) while he works on B-29B tail turret equipped with APG-15, 350 caliber gun radar. (ED HERING)

Colonel Robert Morgan was blessed with the privilege of flying famous airplanes and marking up some firsts in his log books. This was his B-29 *Dauntless Dotty*, at Saipan in which Brig. Gen. Emmett O'Donnell, Commander of the 73rd Wing led the first B-29 raid on Tokyo November 24, 1945. Morgan also was pilot of the *Memphis Bell*, the first B-17 to complete 25 missions against Germany and return to the States. (EVANS)

Colonel Harry Brandon, West Pointer, was promoted to a higher rank and moved to Guam to work in 20th Air Force headquarters early in 1945 after serving as commander of 878th Squadron, 499th Bomb Group. Col. Brandon was killed a few days after the end of the war during a takeoff crash at Guam. He had been associated with the B-29 build-up from the beginning in the Mariana Islands. By the beginning of 1945, bases at Guam and Tinian were well underway to accept four more wings: the 313th at North Field, Tinian; the 314th Wing at North Field, Guam; the 58th Wing which moved from India to West Field, Tinian and 315th Wing at Northwest Field, Guam. Near the end of the war, the 509th Composite Group, the Atomic Bombing Group, came to Tinian to share part of North Field, Tinian with the 313th Wing. (MARSHALL)

B-29 PHOTO COMBAT DIARY

A front shot of a B-29B, clearly showing the highly "secret" new Eagle radar system called the AN/APQ-7. The antenna was housed in an eighteen-foot-wide airfoil-shaped section under the fuselage. The antenna swept from side to side through approximately 60 degrees, and was highly successful. (W.II. KEATHLY, JR.)

Brig. General "Rosey" O'Donnell, center, and Lt. Colonel Robert "Bob" Morgan with head down, talk with news media people after landing from the first B-29 bombing raid on Tokyo November 24, 1944. Morgan and O'Donnell (73rd Wing Commander) led the mission. One hundred-eleven B-29s took off for the mission, ninety-nine made it to the target, and only two planes were lost. (U.S. AIR FORCE PHOTO)

V-46 of the 499th Bomb Group, Saipan flies directly over the cut off cone shaped, tallest mountain in all Japan, Mt. Fuji. The top of the mountain is covered with snow almost year-round. The clipped tail of the cone is scalloped out like someone or something dipped ice cream from it. (MARSHALL)

Five hundred pound clusters of incendiary M-69 bombs leave the bellies of B-29 Superfortresses from the 500th Bomb Group on Saipan. This was a daylight raid, but most fire raid missions took place at night at altitudes from 5,000 to 10,000 feet. (73RD WING)

Captain Ray Brashear of the 878th Squadron, 499th Bomb Group, 73rd Wing Saipan, flying in V-25, takes time out to shoot one of the better photos of some very close formation by Squadron mates in V-32.
(RAY BRASHER)

This photo of the 40th bomb Group maintenance men was taken with Superfort #831, named *Queenie*, at Chakulia, India, before the 58th Wing began the move from bases in India and China to Tinian Island in the Pacific. *Quennie* was lost on a mission to Rangoon December 14, 1944.
(CHANGNON)

B-29 PHOTO COMBAT DIARY

Brig. General Thomas Power, commander of the 314th Wing, based at North Field, had for his personal use the best-dressed Superfortress in the Marianas. Symbols of all four flight Groups and the Service Groups were painted on the nose with updates on the number of missions flown by each Group. (KELCIE TEAGUE)

Early arrival at Tinian Island was Major Julian Dendy, left, and Lt. Comdr. T. J. Paggiani, USN. Dendy and Paggiani pose by *Indian Maid*, of which Dendy is aircraft commander. As was the custom on Tinian, some of the Superforts were honored by proclaimed guardian Seabee units, thus the 67th Seabee logo of numbered dominoes is incorporated in the *Indian Maid* name. (ED HERING)

Bob Kenworthy gets ready to paint nose art on this B-29. Men who had a talent with the paint brush made some good pocket change by dressing up Superforts throughout the island bases at Saipan, Tinian and Guam. (CHANGNON)

Superfort #738 and Ned Baugh's crew at Luliang, China, en route to Tinian. They made the long flight to the Pacific island in April, 1945. (CHANGNON)

Major Charles Weber and crew had no trouble making the flight from Chakulia, India in their *Eight Ball Charlie* during the move to Tinian of the 44th Bomb Squadron, 40th Bomb Group. (L. COPPOLA)

Pictured are B-29Bs from the 16th Bomb Group of the 315th Wing in shakedown formation flight near Guam. The 315th was the last full wing of four Groups to participate in the Superfort assault on Japanese home islands. Arriving in

June of 1945, the 315th was based at Northwest Field, Guam. (ED HERING)

B-29 PHOTO COMBAT DIARY

A Superfortress with a history: *Camel Caravan* was used as a tanker with the 468th BG to transfer gasoline from India to foreign bases in China. General "Blondie" Saunders flew this aircraft, serial #42-7333, from the States to India, and it was the first B-29 to reach the forward bases in China. A maintenance man cleans space to paint another "Hump" mission symbol. The aircraft was  flown back to the States by Major Jack Ladd and crew in December, 1944, after a grand total of forty-four Hump missions. (ALTON EVANS)

Monsoon Goon, serial # 42-93828, shown with an inspection in progress in the 468th Bomb Group, stationed at Kharagpur, India. (AL EVANS)

A flight of Superforts in formation over Japan. The big Circle E on the vertical stabilizers indicates the planes belong to the 504th Bomb Group of the 313th Wing on Tinian. The 504th participated in regular bombing missions as well as the very low level aerial mine missions that played havoc with shipping in Japanese ports and straits around the home islands. The mining project was very instrumental in bringing the Japanese war lords to the surrender table on the USS Battleship *Missouri*, September 2, 1945. (ED HERING)

This is a spectacular view captured from the nose of a 39th Bomb Group B-29 Super-fortress as incendiary bombs drop from the bomb bays of preceed-ing planes on the city of Hiratsuka, Japan, July 16, 1945. One hundred thirty-two B-29s of the 314th Bomb Wing, bases at Guam, dropped 1,163 tons of incendiary bombs from altitudes of 10-15,000 feet, in a day-light raid. Only three planes of the entire strike force failed to drop the bombs on the primary target, which was the urban area of the city. Emergency landings were made by 11 planes on the strike force, at Iwo Jima on the return flight to their home base at North Field, Guam. (U.S. AIR FORCE COMBAT PHOTO)

Wes Palsley, an airplane mechanic with the 500th bomb Group on Saipan, poses in front of a damaged engine and propeller that had been removed from *Pride of the Yankees*. The *Pride* lost two engines over Japan and made it back to Saipan. This was considered an outstanding feat. (WES PALSLEY)

A crowd gathers around *Thumper*, back in the States in August, 1945, after participating in forty combat missions against Japan, at a bond rally. Colonel "Pappy" Haynes, who flew as air-craft commander on many of *Thumper*'s missions with the 499th Bomb Group at Saipan had quite a distinguished Air Force career. He was one the the very few pilots that could claim the distinction of flying combat missions over all three of the enemy capital cities, Berlin, Rome and Tokyo. (EVANS)

B-29 PHOTO COMBAT DIARY

General John H. "Skippy" Davies, commander of the 313th Bomb Wing at Tinian, left, congratulates Captain John Fleming and his crew of *Goin' Jessie*, for not ever having to abort a mission in the record-holding B-29. (CHAUNCEY)

Captain Wm. R. "Bill" Howard poses beside *The Pampered Lady* in India, where he was stationed with the 40th Bomb Group at Chakulia. Note the aircraft had flown nine regular bombing missions and 14 "Hump" supply missions from India to a foreign base in China from where bombing missions originated to hit Japanese targets. Howard was killed in a C-54 crash August 24, 1948, participating in the Berlin Airlift. (HOWARD)

B-29s of the 497th Bomb Group 73rd Wing, based on Saipan, shower another load of incendiaries on Yokohama, Japan. This mission took place in March, 1945. (MARSHALL)

Nose art for arriving Superforts in the Mariana Islands was always in big demand, until authorities suddenly clamped rules and regulations on what could be painted on the aircraft. The 73rd Wing at Saipan, for instance, had all freelance artwork deleted and a Wing symbol, a winged ball and spear, uniformly painted on the nose. Also, the 314th's policy was to have a selected U.S. city's name painted on its special symbol. Also in April, 1945, for better visibility for crew trying to rendezvous with aircraft in their own squadron or group, all aircraft in the 20th Air Force enlarged the letters on vertical stabilizers.

Lucky Lady, in all her glory, flew with the 504th Bomb Group, 313th Wing on Tinian. (EVANS)

The 3rd Photo Recon had a big F painted on the nose to identify its aircraft. Girlie pictures were allowed to remain on the group's aircraft, as shown on *Poison Ivy*, serial number 42-24585. The First Photo Recon Squadron, which served with the 58th Wing in India, and the 3rd Photo Recon Squadron, serving with the Twenty First Bomber Command at Guam, were responsible for aerial photos in areas before a bombing mission to help select suitable targets, and also after the raid to help analyze the results. (EVANS)

One of the early arrivals on Saipan, *Wheel N' Deal*, serial number 42-24604, before the symbol change in nose art, was assigned to the 497th Bomb Group, 73rd Bomb Wing, Twenty-First Bomber Command, Saipan. The veteran had flown twenty two missions when the photo was taken. (EVANS)

Fire in number four engine of this 29th Group, 314th Bomb Wing off North Field, Guam, leaves a trail of smoke over Japan. The propeller has been feathered. (HERING)

This Superfortress sits in its hardstand in the 313th Wing area with a name that reflects the good times back in the States, when everybody was listening to the melody or dancing with someone special. *In The Mood* was named for the song made famous by popular band leader Glen Miller. It had made six bombing missions over Japanese home island when this photo was snapped in 1945. (ED HERING)

When General Wainwright surrendered Corregidor to the Japanese, survivors of the old pre-war 19th Bomb Group, were taken to Cabanatuna POW Camp and assigned to work details building an airfield for the Japanese Navy. The date was May 6, 1942, and it would be over three years before these men were heard from again. At the end of World War II, it was learned that some of the old 19th Bomb Group members had been liberated in a camp in Japan. A crew for the "new" 19th Bomb Group, then serving with the 314th Bomb Wing

on Guam, was dispatched in their Superfort *Slick Chick* to pick up some of the survivors of the 19th and bring them to Guam for a big-time welcome. Included in the group of survivors above was Arthur L Thompson, Jr. fourth from left, kneeling. (THOMPSON)

Black smoke overshadows Mount Surabachi on Iwo Jima when a B-29 Superfortress, returning from a mission to Japan, tries to make an emergency landing. The heavily damaged B-29 veered off the runway on landing and struck another plane on the ground, causing the explosion and fire. P-51 Mustangs rest at Iwo for another escort mission over Japan. (ED HERING)

This B-29B sports ten missions since arriving at Guam to begin operation against oil refineries and fuel storage areas in Japanese home islands. Named *Liberty Belle*, the aircraft was assigned to the 501 Bomb Group, 315th Wing at Guam. (EVANS)

Two members of the ground crew watch their plane from the 16th Bomb Group, 315th Wing at Guam take off for an instrument check and slow timing of the engines after an inspection. (ED HERING)

B-29 PHOTO COMBAT DIARY

O-O-Okla-homa came over to Saipan to join the 498th Bomb Group, 73rd Wing. When this picture was taken, no mission symbols had been painted on that smooth Superfort nose. (EVANS)

Miss Mi Nookie, serial #44-69764 glitters in the hardstand as if she had just rolled off the factory production line at Wichita, Kansas. *Miss Nookie* was assigned to the 9th Bomb Group, 313th Wing on Tinian. (A.O. EVANS)

Flak Alley Sally, serial number 42-24878, of the 6th Bomb Group, 313th Bomb Wing and North Field, Tinian, is shown with early tail markings. The vertical stabilizer later sported a big Circle R. (EVANS)

WORLD WAR II

Weather ahead for these Superforts on way to a target in Japan from the 29th Bomb Group, 314th Bomb Wing on Guam. This was common sight for B-29 crews flying from the Mariana Islands to Japan. Almost always, at least two weather fronts occurred en route, usually between Iwo Jima and Japanese mainland. (HERING)

On May 20, 1945, during take-off for a mine mission to Miyazu and Maizuru Bays near the Shimonoseki Straits in Japan, the 9th Group's *Thunderin' Loretta* was taking off when it exploded, obliterating *Thunderin' Loretta* and destroying two 504th Group B-29s. Lt. William Caldwell and his crew were killed, except the tail gunner, who miraculously survived after escaping from his compartment door and dropping ten feet to the ground before the explosion occurred. (ED HERING)

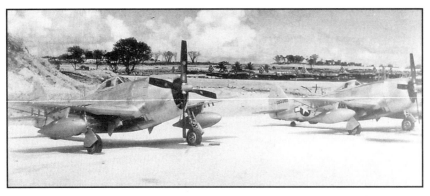

During the battles for the Mariana islands, the P-47 Thunderbolts played an important roll in fighting off Japanese fighter planes during the struggle for the island. These two "thunderbolts" stand by at one of the bases after Saipan, Tinian and Guam were wrested from the Japanese. (ED HERING)

B-29 PHOTO COMBAT DIARY

B-29B Superforts of the 16th Bomb Group, 315th Wing at Guam, stand ready at Northwest Field for a night raid on oil refineries north of Tokyo. (ED HERING)

Superfortresses of the 29th bomb Group, 314 Bomb Wing, rest in the hardstands at North Field on Guam. The big O, inside a black square, assures easy identification of the Group. Regular maintenance takes place between missions. (ED HERING)

North Field on Tinian showing the parking area for the 313th Wing. The nearest planes, with the Circle R, belong to the 6th Bomb Group. At the extreme right is a Circle Arrow, which is

one of the modified aircraft of the 509th Composite Group, the atomic bombing group. North Field was, at the time, the world's largest airfield. It had four parallel runways over 8,000 feet long. The mountain in the background is on Saipan, where the 73rd Wing was located. The channel between the two islands was about 3 miles wide. (K. PATTISON)

This *Sentimental Journey*, assigned to the 444th Bomb Group, 58th Wing, saw duty against Japanese targets from bases in Dudkhundi, India, and Kwanghan, China, as well as West Field on Tinian, just three miles across the channel from Saipan. (A.O. EVANS)

Captain Bill Hunter, front row, left, and his crew, flying *Bombin' Buggy II*, claim to be among the very first B-29s to reach the target at Yawata, Japan, on Kyushu, one of the three main home islands, on June 5, 1944. The raid was the first B-29 mission against mainland Japan. The crew was assigned to the 40th Bomb Group, 59th Bomb Wing, bases at Chakulia, India. (EVANS)

McLaren crew, both the flight and ground crews, of the 40th Bomb Group, pose by *Miss You* at the West Field, Tinian, after their move from India. (WEMPLE)

B-29 PHOTO COMBAT DIARY

V Square 60, with the unusual name of *Umbriago III—Dat's My Boy*, lies afloating in a watery grave. Sy Sylvester and crew of the 878th Squadron, 499th Bomb Group, was using the 879th Squadron plane for a mission to Nagoya. They made it back within 60 miles of Saipan before ditching because of fuel shortage. All crew members escaped the plane and spent 17 hours in rubber

boats before the USS *Cummins* picked them up. The plane was still floating and over forty shells were fired into the plane before sinking it. (SYLVESTER)

Standing in front of their aircraft, *Umbriago III—Dat's My Boy*, in the 879th Bomb Squadron, 499th Bomb Group, is part of the regular crew of the plane. They lost their plane however, December 12, 1944, when Lt. Sylvester and crew ditched it returning to Saipan from an airplane engine plant at Nagoya. (SYLVESTER)

A gunner on *Million Dollar Baby II* checks and loads the forward top turret prior to a mission. Note the four .50-caliber machine guns, which are fired by remote control by the gunner sitting in the center department several feet away. The *Baby* belonged to the 468th Bomb Group, 58th Wing on West Field, Tinian. Bomb symbols show the aircraft had made 20 missions. (DEARDORFF)

WORLD WAR II

35

West Field, on Tinian, was built after North Field, on Tinian, to accommodate the 58th Wing's four Groups, after completing business in India and China, and coming to the Mariana Islands to join in the all-out assault on Japan's home islands. The base was built on the west side of Tinian about midway across the island. This scene is looking east. (CHANGNON)

The mechanic's work was never done. Here, two of the ground crewmen, in the 500th Bomb Group on Saipan, prepare to change an engine. You can see they had to remove the cowling after removing the big four bladed propellers, before the real work begins. (SPEITH)

B-29 PHOTO COMBAT DIARY

The author's crew: left to right, standing: John W. Cox, A/C; Chester Marshall, pilot; John Huckins, Flight Engineer; Jim O'Donnel, navigator; Herbert Feldman, bombardier. Kneeling: Robert Slisuski, radar; Alvin Torres, radio; Kendal Chance, CFC; George Koepke, right gunner; Arle Lacky, left gunner; and John Sutherland, tail gunner. The crew was in the 878th Squadron, 499th Bomb Group, at Saipan. Photo was taken June 8, 1944, one day after com-

pleting a 30 mission combat tour. Flag symbols represent 10 Japanese fighters shot down. The bomb bay symbol, between bombs, represents the day we dropped bombbay fuel over Tokyo, when bomb release mechanization froze and we had to salvo bombs to clear the bombays over Tokyo. (MARSHALL)

This is not the "Fat Man" atomic bomb that leveled Nagaski, but one thing is for sure, this baby carries a wallop. And it's not a one man job to load it into a Superfortress. The armament man, sitting atop this 2,000 pound demolition bomb, waits for some strong help to load it into a Superfort. (SPEITH)

Stanley Poplaski and crew pose by their Superfort, *The Outlaw*, at West Field, Tinian. When this picture was taken, *The Outlaw*, had completed twenty missions over Japanese targets. (POPLASKI)

Dark Slide was a photo plane with the 3rd Photo Recon Squadron at Guam. The original B-29s that the 3rd Photo used were modified B-29As and retained the gun turrets, because fighter opposition was much more aggressive than later on when fire raids and B-29s, in the 315th Wing on Guam, with the new "Eagle" radar units, destroyed most of Japans fuel storage and refineries. (MITCHELL)

The armament crew of the 485th Bomb Squadron, 16th Bomb Group, 315th Wing at Northwest Field, Guam, are ready to start loading these 500 pound demolition bombs in the double bombays of another Superfort. Picture, left to right: Williams, Hering, Dahl, Acrieri, Scjpbert and Maxworthy. (ED HERING)

This classic photo was taken on Iwo Jima just before pilots of the P-51s of the 21st Fighter Group prepared to take off for an escort mission over Japan. The three story high vertical stabilizer of #19, a B-29 Superfortress, called a "mother ship," stationed at Iwo, was used to accompany the fighter to and from Iwo to relieve the fighter pilots from navigating individually on the 1,400 mile trip. (CURTIS)

B-29 PHOTO COMBAT DIARY

Close forma-
tion—this flight
of Superforts
from the 9th
Bomb Group,
313th Wing at
Tinian, head
for a target on
Honshu, Japan
for a daylight
raid. On night
incendiary
raids, later in
the war, after
Iwo Jima was
taken, elimi-
nating enemy
attacks from
that island en route from the Marianas to Japan, B-29 crews flew to and from the target and
over the target individually, not in formation. (DOTY)

Black smoke boils from this aircraft from the 504th Bomb Group, 313th Wing at Tinian, after
it veered too close to the edge of the runway during the takeoff and struck another aircraft.
Exploding bombs, along with gasoline, made the smoke so dense, it was easily seen across the
channel on Saipan. (A.R. SAEZ)

20th Century Sweetheart is being readied for another raid on a target in Japan. The *Sweetheart* sits in her hardstand in the 500th Bomb Group, 73rd Wing at Isley Field on Saipan. (HASSELL)

Two maintenance men from the 498th Bomb Group, 73rd Wing, at Isley Field, Saipan, replace a damaged rudder on T Square 44. Note the long barrel protruding from the tail gun turret. The early B-29s in the Pacific had a 20MM cannon, along with two .50-caliber machine guns, but trouble occurred often when the cannon was used, because of jamming. Eventually, the cannon was removed, leaving the machine guns, but some of the tail gunners flew missions for a while with a stick protruding to try and fool attacking fighters. (CURTIS)

Jim Handwerker and crew brought *The City of Memphis* all the way back from Japan to Guam on two good engines. A lot of smoke and dust accompanied the landing. Jim was awarded the Silver Star for the feat. The big M on the tail indicated plane was with the 19th Bomb Group, 314th Bomb Wing. (HANDWERKER)

B-29 PHOTO COMBAT DIARY

From this photo, you'd think these two B-29 Superfortresses were playing like they were dive bombers. In reality, however, it's more like the developer of the negative did a little realignment on his enlarging machine. (P. DALY)

This is the control tower that served the 315th Wing at Northwest Field. The Traffic Controllers at B-29 bases in the Mariana Islands, and at Iwo Jima, did outstanding jobs in directing traffic, sometimes under extremely difficult situations. Through their efforts many crews, about to run out of gas or in damaged aircraft, were nursed in for landings. (ED HERING)

Harry Changnon was flying copilot on *Patches* of the 40th bomb Group, Tinian, when this near-disaster occurred on return to Tinian after a raid on Tokyo, May 26, 1945. (CHANGNON)

A near-disaster occurred when brakes failed on #396, while trying to land a heavily damaged aircraft at Tinian's West Field. (CHANGNON)

When the 58th Wing came to Tinian in the spring of 1945, its runways at West Field were ready to receive aircraft, but permanent-type living quarters were not yet finished. Everybody, ground crews, flight crews, including officers and enlisted men, had to sleep in tents. The 40th

Bomb Group's living area, shown above, was located down near the water. (CHANGNON)

This B-29, with the name of *The Life of Riley*, sparkles with a bubbling "shady lady" ready to party. The plane was one of the 504th Bomb Group, 313th Wing, at North Field, Tinian. (ED HERING)

Superfort #859 leads a three-plane element over the Sumitoma Metals Plant in a daylight raid at Osaka, on May 24, 1945. The 40th Bomb Group received its 3rd Presidential Unit Citation for its outstanding bombing of this target. (CHANGNON)

A gunner, top right, prepares the four .50-caliber machines and turret for a mission. *Jackpot*, with bold art work, rests in a hardstand in the 505th Bomb Group, 313th Wing, at North Field, Tinian. (HERING)

Hore-zontal Dream was also an early arrival to the Marianas from India. The Superfortress was with the 676th Squadron, 444th Bomb Group. The Squadron ensignia, "Disney's Reluctant Dragon," appeared on the noses of most of Squadron's airplanes. (CHANGNON)

WORLD WAR II

Incendiary bombs spew from the bombays of P#34 of the 39th Bomb Group, 314th Wing, based at North Field, Guam. This was a daylight raid on one of the major cities in Japan. (MARSHALL)

This aircraft was a B-29B, with the 331st Bomb Group, 315th Wing, on Northwest Field, Guam. Note, this model had no gun turrets, and the only machine guns aboard were the twin .50-caliber tail guns. Her name: *Pom Pom*. (EVANS)

This photo shows the twin 8,800 feet runways at Isley Field, home of the 73rd Bomb Wing, 21st Bomber Command, Saipan. The scene also shows most of the living area of the personnel along Obyan Coast on the Southern tip of Saipan. (73RD WING PHOTO)

Nose art on this Superfort, which flew with the 462nd Bomb Group, 58th Wing, at Tinian, stressed the fact that *Iron George* always carried a heavy load. When photo was taken, the plane had made eleven strikes against Japan from Tinian. (HENRY)

Captain Ray Brashear looks out his cockpit window to check smoke coming from number two engine, during an engine check. This photo was shot after Brashear and crew had completed 14 missions with the 878th Squadron, 499th Bomb Group at Saipan. Gunners on the crew had three Japanese kills at the time. (BRASHEAR)

Major J.L. Carr, and his crew, on *Satan's Lady* with the 504th Bomb Group, 313th Wing, at Saipan, commissioned a Marine named Scott to paint the nose art on the plane. Scott was always in demand to paint girlie pictures on the Superforts. Some of his better artwork appeared on *Dinah Might*, *Island Queen* and *Good Deal*, all in the 504th Group.

In June, 1945, General Frank Armstrong, commander of the 315th Bomb Wing, based at Northwest Field, Guam, announced that the 501st Bomb Group would be providing an aircraft to be dedicated to Admiral Chester Nimitz, in recognition of the logistical support the Navy had given the B-29s. Colonel Boyd Hubbard, of the 501st Group, was directed to select the plane for the ceremonies. On June 15, 1945, General Hap Arnold, Commanding Officer of the Army Air Force, was on hand for the presentation to Admiral Nimitz. Shown standing beneath the B-29B, newly named *Fleet Admiral Nimitz*, with Admiral's five-star flag painted on it were, from left: Admiral Nimitz, Colonel Hubbard, and General Hap Arnold. (MARSHALL)

The *Smokey Stover* crew lines up for a photo. Stationed at Chakulia, India with the 40th Bomb Group, in 1944. Left to right, front row: Jones, Offerman, Copley, Smith and Perry. Rear, left to right: Whitley, McDaniel, Danks, Conant, Melomine and Morend. (CHANGNON)

These two Generals, Wing commanders, "Rosey" O'Donnell, 73rd Wing, Saipan, left, and General Davies, 313th Wing, Tinian, meet for a relaxed conversation, which most assuredly included some serious policy talk, at Tinian. The date: early 1945. (MARSHALL)

The Cajun Queen, with eighteen missions over Japan, with the 444th Bomb Group, 58th Wing, based at West Field on Tinian. The crew of this ship liked the

Seabees so well, the nose art includes the 110th NCB Battalion. (F. HENRY/CHANGNON)

The Agitator II, another veteran from the CBI Theatre, made the move from India to Tinian in April, 1945. The "Reluctant Dragon" insignia of the 676th Bomb Squadron, 444th Bomb Group, gets ready to add another mission symbol to its long line of symbols on its nose.
(HOUGDAHL)

Jokers Wild, serial number 42-24626, was an early arrival with the 497th Group at Saipan. Orders were issued by 73rd Wing officials, (we never did find out who), to remove all nose art from B-29s belonging to the 73rd, after which a uniform Wing ensignia of a winged ball and a long spear, on which the aircraft's name could be painted. It took away some of the originalty of the crews. (EVANS)

WORLD WAR II

Top "brass" in the Marianas, early 1945. This strategy meeting took place at Saipan soon after the arrival of Colonel, later General, Power, and his 314th Wing at Guam. From left: General "Possum" Hansell, CO of the XXIst Bomber Command; Colonel Power, CO of 314th Wing; Colonel,

later General Davies, CO of 313th Wing at Tinian, and General Ramey, Deputy CO, XXIst Bomber Command. (HANSELL)

An aerial view of Northwest Field at Guam, home of the 315th Bomb Wing. It was the last of the five big bases built to accommodate the five Wings of the XXIst Bomber Command. (HERING)

A group of B-29s from the 499th Bomb Group, 73rd Wing, Saipan, in tight formation, head for a target in Japan. Captian Ray Brashear, airplane commander of V-25 (engine in foreground) snapped this picture of an 878th Squadron mate. (BRASHEAR)

B-29 PHOTO COMBAT DIARY

Slick Dick arrived on Saipan in late October, 1944, with the 500th Bomb Group, 73rd Wing, and after some practice strikes against Truk, participated in the first B-29 raid on Tokyo, November 24, 1945. (WITT)

Among the first group of B-29 Superfortresses to get to the Mariana Islands, *Black Magic*, with the 500th Bomb Group, 73rd Wing, at Isley Field, Saipan, participated in the first B-29 raid on Tokyo, November 24, 1944. (SPEITH)

Showing some unusual nose art and symbols, *Ready Betty*, served with the 468th Bomb Group, 58th Wing, in India-China, before the move to Tinian in April and May of 1945. The aircraft serial number was 42-24879. (EVANS)

WORLD WAR II

A most beautiful sight from the cockpit of a B-29 Superfortress heading toward landfall and a target in Japan. The Superforts were without fighter escorts over Japan until Iwo Jima was captured in March, 1945. The first Mustang escort mission took place April 7, 1945. (MARSHALL)

Captain Richard, left, bombardier; Major Marvin Goodwyn, aircraft commander; and Captain Donal Manfredo, navigator, check the map to make sure they understand the charted route to and from the target. They are members of 40th Bomb Group. (CHANGNON)

Strategy talk at Saipan among three leaders in the B-29 Superfortress operation in December, 1944. Paying close attention to maps spread out on the hood of a Jeep in the 497th Bomb Group area, 73rd Wing, are from left: General Emmett O'Donnell, 73rd Wing Commander; General Harman, Deputy Commanding General of the Twentieth Air, with headquarters still in Washington; and General Haywood Hansell, CO of the XXIst Bomber Command. (HANSELL)

B-29 PHOTO COMBAT DIARY

One of the big guns the Japanese left behind on Saipan. The airman makes it appear that he is about to load and lock a live shell. To the left of the gun barrel, you see in the distance, B-29s at Isley Field. (PASLEY)

Shanghai Lil Rides Again of the 444th bomb Group, was one of the first planes of the 58th Wing to make the move from India to Tinian. The crew flew with the 6th Bomb Group of the 313th Wing on Tinian of the April 13 Tokyo mission. Serial # of *Lil* was #42-6277. (EVANS)

Busy days at Iwo Jima for the mechanics. Planes from several Groups and Wings of B-29s in the Marianas await repair jobs, including changing of engines shown lined up on ground near parking area. The Black square O belonged to the 29th Bomb Group, 314th Wing at Guam. Others identified were the Big Z of the 500th Group, 73rd Wing Saipan, Big T, 497th Group, Saipan, and Circle E from the 504th Group, Tinian. (ED HERING)

Ed Hering, squatting with fire extinguisher, is fire guard on engine #4, as plane from the 16th Bomb Group, 315th Wing at Guam, starts up for a mission on oil refineries in Japan. (HERING)

Signs points to the headquarters building of the Twentieth Air Force at Guam. Originally, the Twentieth Air Force five Wings received orders from Washington, but after the entire command moved to the Mariana Islands, so did the headquarters operations. (HERING)

P-51 Mustangs line up along the taxi strip at Iwo Jima, ready to taxi out for a long range escort mission over targets in Japan, 700 miles away. The engines are running, and the extra fuel tanks under the wings are full, and the pilots are ready to go. A B-29 "mother ship" will navigate the 1,500 round trip for the Mustang pilots. (MARSHALL)

B-29 PHOTO COMBAT DIARY

Like the Super-forts in the 504th Group, with a reputation of having some of the snazziest nose art in the Pacific, the crews of the 505th Group came up with some good girlie artwork to decorate their Super-fort, like this one named *Pacific Playboys.*
(RILEY)

Rush Order was a real veteran, having served with the 462nd Bomb Group, 58th Wing, based at Piardoba, India, with many "Hump" missions over the Himalayan Mountains, as well as bombing missions from China and also Tinian.
(CHANGNON)

Lt. Thomas A. Bell's crew pose for picture by their *City of Maywood* on the flight line at North Field, Guam. They flew with the 60th Squadron, 39th Bomb Group, 314th Wing. Front row, left to right: Sgts. Tom Smith, tail gunner; John Essig, CFC gunner; David Schulman. radio; George Beaver, Flight Engineer; David Potter, left gunner; and Ralph Johnson, right gunner. Rear, left to right: Lts. Charles Baldridge, bombardier; Richard D. Harrison, CP; Thomas Bell, AC; Elmer Jones, radar, and Joseph E. Callaghan, navigator. (JONES)

WORLD WAR II   53

This picture of the Major Eddie Glass Crew of the 395th Squadron, 40th Bomb Group, was taken just before the plane went down, returning to India from a forward base in China. The crew disappeared somewhere over the "Hump." (CHANGNON)

Captain Everett Berry, and crew with the 44th Bomb Squadron, 40th Bomb Group, based at Chakulia, India, pose for this picture, September 1, 1944. (CHANGNON)

Major Joseph D. White, and crew, with the 40th Bomb Group, 59th Wing in India, pose for this picture at the nose of their B-29 *San Antonio Rose*. (S. LAUBE)

B-29 PHOTO COMBAT DIARY

This is an unusual picture of Mt. Fuji, Japan's tallest mountain peak, located about 60 miles southwest of Tokyo. What makes this shot so unusual is there is very little snow, only a small amount, on the very tip of the peak. Most of the time, even in summer, snow was more plentiful near the top of the 12,300-plus foot mountain. Superfort number 22, of the 19th Bomb Group, with the big Square M, makes a good picture, framed in a small cloud bank, with Fuji in the background. (JOE PRESCOTT)

Bill Renfro's crew at their base in India, flew with 564th Squadron, 40th Bomb Group, 58th Wing, in *Ding How*. The aircraft shows 17 supply mission were flown across the "Hump," three more than the 14 bombing missions flown when this picture was taken. (RENFRO)

Among the white fluffy clouds, flight formation of B-29s from the 314th Wing at Guam, paint a pretty picture, as viewed over the tail section of a B-29 parked in the 29th bomb Group area at North Field, Guam. (PRESCOT)

All dressed up for battle in the skies over Japan. This photo of a fellow crewman in the 6th Squadron, 29th Bomb Group at Guam, was snapped by pilot Joe Prescott. Pictured is the two-piece flak suit and steel strips, covered by cloth, which was not very comfortable. In addition, crew members were required to wear a Mae West life jacket that inflated by pulling a plug fit around the chest, and would keep a person afloat. (PRESCOTT)

Soon after this picture was taken of Major Alex Zamry, 395th Squadron, 40th Bomb Group, on June 1, 1944, the crew had to ditch their plane returning from a mission against a Japanese target. Killed in the ditching were Major Zamry and three crew members. (CHANGNON)

B-29 PHOTO COMBAT DIARY

Black Square K 30 from the 330th bomb Group, 314th Wing, from Guam, cruises casually on its way to Japan. The plane is flying at a relatively low altitude to preserve fuel on the way to the target. Lots of extra fuel had to be used to climb  with a heavy load aboard. It was therefore urgent that the planes fly most of the way up to Japan at low altitudes, making it less fuel consuming to climb to bombing altitudes. (PRESCOTT)

 Another scene of Mount Fuji, showing the way the top of mountain usually looked with a large blanket of snow reaching down the mountain side. A pretty scene looking between two Superforts from the 29th Bomb Group, Guam. (PRESCOTT)

Pictured here is the entire Maintenance force in the 16th Bomb Group, whose service was absolutely essential before a B-29 could leave the ground. Grouped in front of and standing on the wings of two Superforts were the men who kept them flying. Pictured are the mechanics, the specialists, and the men who loaded the bombs and ammunition. (HERING)

WORLD WAR II

57

The 502nd Bomb Group, 315th Wing, had two significant distinctions recorded as the part they played in the B-29 assault against Japan. Pictured, is the first Superfort, #263, to land at Guam in the 315th Wing. The date was June 22, 1945. The other historical distinction for the 502nd Group is the fact that a B-29B flown by Captain Robert Trask, *The Uninvited*, had engine trouble and was very late getting off on the Akita Oil Refinery mission led by Wing Commander General Armstrong. Nevada Lee, who was the 502nd flight line maintenance officer that night, still has documented evidence verifying the departure time and return from mission. Trask was credited with dropping the last bomb on Japan the night of August 15th, when WWII ended. (HERING)

Approaching Isley Field, Saipan, this Superfort enters traffic pattern flying in a southward direction. The final approach will be made from the west. The prevailing wind at Isley Field was almost always from the east, so landings and takeoffs were made to the east. (SPEITH)

B-29 PHOTO COMBAT DIARY

This flight of B-29s from the 498th Bomb Group, 73rd Wing, Siapan, heads into landfall and will use Mount Fuji, upper left, for the IP (initial point) to line up on the bomb run toward a target in Tokyo, 60-70 miles away. (73RD WING PHOTO)

Lt. Crow and Lt. Turner, of the 500th Bombardment Group, 73rd Wing, 21st Bomber Command, pose beside a wrecked Japanese tank in a jungle battlefield at Saipan. (U.S. AIR FORCE PHOTO)

Major Baugh's Superfort #37, on hardstand, at West Field, Tinian, with the 40th Bomb Group. The picture was taken August 15, 1945, the day of the Japanese

capitulation, and the war was over. As you can tell by the "Hump," and regular bombing mission symbols, she was a veteran of both CBI and Pacific Theaters. (L. COIRA)

Another unusual shot of Mount Fuji, Honshu's tallest mountain peak. This Superfort, and those with him, on this daylight mission, is about to make his turn on the bomb run to the right toward the target in Toyko. The aircraft appears to be flying at almost the same altitude as the height of Fuji, just over 12,300 feet. (KELCIE TEAGUE)

A typical bomb dump on the Mariana Islands, stacked neatly awaiting to be loaded into the double bays of the Superfortresses. This storage dump was at Saipan. (SPEITH)

The Twentieth Century Limited arrived at Saipan in early December, 1944, and was commanded by Captain Tull K. McGuire. The plane flew fifty-one missions with the 881st Bomb Squadron, 500th Bomb Group, surviving the war. McGuire, and his crew, were lost when they ditched another aircraft, Z-13, after bombing Tokyo. (HURTH THOMKINS)

B-29s from the 16th Bomb Group, 315th Wing, off of Guam, proceed toward their target in Japan, which was probably some oil refinery. All four groups of the 315th flew the B-29B, modified to illuminate all turrets except the tail gunner position. His guns were fired direct, not by remote control like guns on the regular B-29s. (HERING)

What a sight it was to see a flight of B-29s salvo their heavy loads of 500-pound clusters of incendiary bombs on targets in Japan. Pilots had to be very cautious when controlling their aircraft when a heavy load of bombs were salvoed. The airplane, it seemed, handled like a bucking bronco set free, trying to climb up, up and away. (73RD WING PHOTO)

Omaha One More Time flew with the 9th Bomb Group, 313th Bomb Wing, and participated in some of the low level mine laying missions in the Shimonoseki Straits, between Honshu and Kyushu Islands. Aerial mines dropped in ports and Straits around the main islands of Japan were very effective, tying up most of their shipping. (HERING)

Mount Surabatchi was located at the southern tip of a seven mile long gourd-shaped island of Iwo Jima. It was here where the picture of the raising of the Stars and Stripes produced one of the classic photos of World War II. In the hardest fought battle at that time in WWII, the Marines lost 4,590 men killed, plus 301 declared missing and 15,954 wounded, in the battle for Iwo Jima, which lasted from February 19, 1945 to March 16, 1945. (MARSHALL)

The 2nd Army's Repair Unit Ship, called *Noah's Ark*, is shown at Iwo Jima after moving up from Saipan after the island was captured. The ship was literally a floating repair shop, with all the necessary machinery to make parts quickly for B-29s on the spot rather than having to get parts shipped in or flown in from the Unit-

ed States. The ship had two helicopters aboard for ship to shore delivery. The helicopters were the fourth and fifth ever commissioned for the U.S. Air Force. Captain William B. Gassaway was the Air Force commander of a 32 man gun crew aboard the ship. (ED HERING)

Technicians on the 2nd Army Unit Ship, anchored off Iwo Jima, after moving up from Saipan when Iwo Jima was captured, worked around the clock, making parts for B-29s and P-51s. Keeping them in the air, rather than having to wait for parts shipped in from the States, played a big part in winning the war against Japan. (ED HERING)

Ernie Pyle, center at table, visits with friends while visiting in the 500th Group, 499th Bomb Group, on his way to cover the war taking place at Okinawa early in 1945. Ernie was the most popular war correspondent in World War II. He was loved by all branches of service and covered most of the major battlegrounds, in the trenches with the foot soldier,

in Europe and the Pacific. Two weeks after this picture was taken, he was killed by a sniper's bullet, on a small island called Ie Shima, near the big island of Okinawa. (SPEITH)

The 3rd Photo Recon Squadron at Guam, later joined by the First Photo Recon that had been supporting the 58th Wing Bomber Command in CBI Theater, did an outstanding job of photographing almost the entire home islands of Japan. From these photos, targets could easily be identified for bombing missions. After every raid, pictures were taken of the bombed areas for analysis by the planners. (EVANS)

This photo was taken of *Adam's Eve* in about January, 1945, before the 73rd Wing's policy makers declared girlie nose art null and void and had it all removed from the four Groups' B-29s. *Adam's Eve* flew with the 500th Bomb Group. Her serial number was 42-24600. (EVANS)

WORLD WAR II

According to a story in the June 5, 1945 issue of *Brief*, the magazine that covered the comings and goings and outstanding feats of Air Force people throughout the Pacific, John Sutherland, tail gunner on the J. W. Cox crew #25, on which the author was a pilot, was the leading B-29 gunner in the 20th Air Force B-29 operation in the Pacific. Sutherland was credited with five verified kills and two probables, which put him ahead of all B-29 gunners, according to the article. In fighter pilot jargon, five kills meant he was the only B-29 gunner ace. (MARSHALL)

A close runner-up to John Sutherland for top gunner in B-29s was T/Sgt. Anthony F. Migliaccio, Central Fire Control gunner on Colonel "Pappy" Hayne's crew in the 499th Bomb Group on Saipan. Toney is pictured standing on top of his aircraft *Thumper*. (MIGLIACCIO)

Lt. Leslie Hodson, third from right, front, and crew, smile for the camera while at dinghy practice, which is learning how to get into a life raft. The exercises were mandatory for B-29 crews who had to fly up to 3,000 mile round trips on missions to Japan. Some of the men have inflated their "Mae West" life jackets. With missions of up to 3,000 miles round trip over water, all crew members were anxious to get in some practice—it could very well come in handy. (MARSHALL)

The Darrel McGuffey crew was one of the first replacement crews to join the 878th Squadron, 499th Bomb Group, on Saipan. Almost from the the start of the operation against Japan from the Mariana Islands, replacements were needed for a big number of crews lost by enemy action or by ditching in the ocean on the way home. McGuffey is pictured standing on the left. (MARSHALL)

Results of a ramming tactic by a Japanese fighter pilot. Colonel Morris Lee, 499th Group commander, was flying in this airplane from the 878th Squadron over Kobe on June 5, 1945, when a head-on fighter attack clipped the horizontal stabilizer. Captain Ray Brashear brought the plane all the way back to Isley Field, Saipan without too much difficulty. (HART)

Lt. Eugene Parrish, and crew, pose for a picture before leaving the Herrington, Kansas staging base for the Pacific. The crew arrived at Saipan early in February and was assigned to the 878th Squadron, 499th Group. They replaced an unfortunate crew that ditched on an earlier mission. The Parrish crew was still flying missions when hostilities ended August 15, 1945, and participated in flying supplies to POW camps in Japan. (MARSHALL)

Circle R, #3, of the 6th bomb Group, 313th Wing, at North Field, Tinian, three miles across the channel from the southern tip of Saipan, flies low over one of the small islands that were part of the Mariana Islands chain. The Big Circle R was probably the most famous Group tail emblem to come out of World War II. The reason: This was the identification insignia that was painted on the tail surface of the *Enola Gay*, the airplane that dropped the atomic bomb on Hiroshima. That plane was with the 509th Composite Group and that Group's insignia was a Circle Arrowhead. Col. Paul Tibbets had the R painted on it to maybe fool the Japanese. (MATTHEW HEGERLE)

Ground crewmen had a lot of work to do on *Pride of the Yankees* when Lt. Frank "Chico" Carrico, and crew, brought the plane back to Isley Field's 500th Bomb Group with two engines out after the daylight raid on the Musashino aircraft plant (target #357) in suburbs of Tokyo, January 27, 1945. Fighters that day were extremely aggressive against the 76 plane strike from the 73rd Wing's four Groups. Nine B-29s from the Wing were lost, and several received serious damage. The two replacement engines are ready to be installed on the *Pride*. (PASLEY)

B-29 PHOTO COMBAT DIARY

These hardworking ground crewmen had to go on round the clock shifts to put the *Pride* back in the air in record time. This would not be the last time *Pride of the Yankees* had to return to Saipan from a mission to Japan on two engines. On a later mission, Captain Cecil Tackett brought her back with both outboard engines out. The *Pride* was the only B-29 on Saipan to make the trip home twice on two engines. The January 27th mission would be the last one to Japan as the only B-29 Wing attacking home islands from

the Marianas. The 313th Wing at Tinian had completed two shake down missions, one against Truk, January 21, and one against Iwo Jima, January 24. From here on out more and more Superforts would join in the final assault on Japan. (HAROLD ALFORD)

Mechanics prepare engine mount to replace one of the 2,200 HP Wright engines lost on the January 27, 1945 raid on the Musashino airplane factory at Tokyo. Lt. Garrico and crew of *Pride of the Yankees* reported that a Japanese fighter, called a "Tony," made a head-on attack from above, just as they were releasing bombs, and riddled the #2 engine. The propeller was damaged and would not feather. Soon the run-away prop finally burned off and flew into the propeller of engine #1, putting it out of commission. Luckily the crew made it back on just two good engines, both on the same side. (WES PASLEY)

Disaster struck in the 44th Squadron, 40th Bomb Group, at Chakulia, India, January 14th, 1945, with two B-29s destroyed, and several more damaged. Nine ground crew members were killed and 21 injured when fragment bombs were accidentally dropped to concrete, causing them to explode. The Squadron's B-29s were loaded for a mission using frag bombs when orders came down to change the type

of bombs to be carried on the strike. The resulting deaths and damage was considered the worst accidental disaster to happen to the 20th AF B-29s during the war. (CHANGNON)

One of the most dreaded mishaps that could happen to a B-29 crew would be a forced ditching going to or from a mission to Japan. Before Iwo Jima was captured in March 1945, making it possible to land damaged aircraft that could not make it back to their Mariana bases, numerous crews were lost in ditching their B-29s in the ocean. The first ditching of a crew in the author's 878th Squadron, 499th Group on Saipan, happened to the Sy Sylvester's crew returning from the December 13, 1944 strike against Nagoya. After running out of fuel about 60 miles north of Saipan, Sy made a perfect dead stick landing. All eleven men escaped without too much trouble and after securing the three life rafts from the still floating aircraft, pulled away from the airplane, and safely in the rafts, settled down for the night. Seventeen hours later the aircraft was still floating and the crew was anxiously searching the skies for some help to show up. Finally, at about 2 PM, after spending 17 hours in the water on rafts, a Navy PBY found them. They notified the nearest ship which was the USS *Cummings* who rushed to pick up Sy's Crew. The above picture shows the crew in rafts awaiting to be picked up by the *Cummings*. (SYLVESTER)

A rescue team from the USS *Cummings* entered the water to assist putting the downed Sy Sylvester crew aboard the destroyer. The B-29 was still afloat and showed no signs of sinking and the captain of the ship was not about to leave a big Superfortress floating around in the open ocean. He decid-

ed to sink the plane. It took over forty 40MM shells to sink the plane. In the meantime, another 878th crew, with Lt. Ledbetter at the controls, with major damage and running out of fuel when they reached Saipan, was forced to make a second pass at the runway due to the crowded traffic pattern of B-29s trying desperately to get on solid ground after a hectic time over Japan that day. The plane crashed just off the end of the runway killing all aboard. (SYLVESTER)

This Superfort with the 6th Bomb Group is getting all four engines changed at the same time, which was unusual for engine change operations at Tinian. But this time it's for a special occasion. Note the sign underneath the wing. This was taking place soon after the Japanese capitulation August 15. B-29s from Saipan, Tinian, and Guam were scheduled to search for POW Camps where the Japanese would be holding American and Allied soldiers and airmen all over Japan and as far away as Korea, Manchuria and China. Once located, Superforts loaded with food, medicine and all kinds of supplies, would drop them by parachutes tied to 55-gallon drums. (MATTHEW HEGERLE)

Mis-Chief-Maker, #42-24896, joined the 462nd Bomb Group at West Field, Tinian in the spring of 1945, after the four Groups of the XXth Bomber Command moved from bases in India to West Field, Tinian. After shake-down missions to Truk, and other by-passed islands, she made her first mission to Hiro, located in Honshu, the main island in Japan. After the XX Bomber Command's Groups made the move to the Marianas, it was disbanded and consumed by the XXIst bomber Command under which all the B-29s Groups then operated under one Bomber Command. (EVANS)

This picture was not taken over Hiroshima or Nagasaki. It is a photo of Tokyo after the March 9/10 fire raid by regular B-29s—324 of them, from the three Wings, 73rd, 313th and 314th. Each B-29 unloaded an average of eight tons of incendiaries on the northeastern section of Tokyo. Seventeen square miles of the city was flattened, except a scattering of a few concrete buildings. Observers there, after the fighting was over, said most of those buildings were gutted. Two million people were left homeless. Other cities would feel a similar fate. Why the Japanese would continue the war was a big mystery to most of us who were there. (J.B. HUDSON)

Colonel Kenneth H. Gibson, left, Commanding Officer of the 6th Bomb Group, 313th Wing, at Tinian, presents the Distinguished Flying Cross to J.B. (Joe) Hudson. Hudson was the radar operator on the Ed Russell crew number 3909. The B-29 they flew was named *Reamatroid*. The presentation of the medal took place in May, 1945. (J.B. HUDSON)

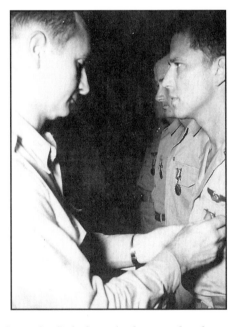

Ed Russell, Airplane Commander of *Reamatroid*. His flight crew number was 3909, with the 6th Bomb Group at North Field, Tinian. The picture was made on the flight line. At the time the photo was made his crew had completed 10 missions against several targets on Honshu, the main island of Japan. The Group was one of the oldest in the 20th Air Force. The coat of arms was first designed and approved for the Sixth in 1924. The insignia of the pirate's head and crest was first used by the 6th Composite Group in Panama, and was reassigned to the Sixth Bombardment Group on February 4, 1943. (J.B. HUDSON)

B-29 PHOTO COMBAT DIARY

Flight crew members of the 6th Bomb Group dressed up in their cleanest khakis to receive earned medals. This presentation was made April 23, 1945, by Brig. General John H. Davies, Commanding Officer of the 313th Bomb Wing on Tinian. The Air Medal was awarded to all XXI Bomber Command flight crewmen after the first five combat missions flown, and an Oak Leaf Cluster after every additional five missions to Japan. (J.B. HUDSON)

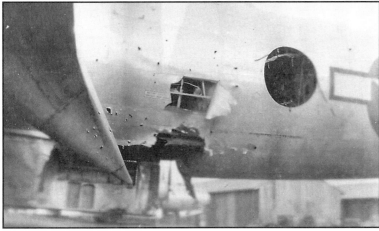

The large holes pictured in the fuselage of this 6th Bomb Group B-29 were results of a direct flak hit over the city of Kobe, during which Charlie Magnuson and Raymon Merritt were killed. Kobe was a heavily industrialized medium-sized city on the northwestern side of Osaka Bay. Like the city of Osaka, which sprawled around the Bay almost reaching Kobe, the anti-aircraft guns were most effective and put up one of the strongest flak defenses in Japan. (J.B. HUDSON)

This flying engine belongs to a B-29 Superfortress en route to its base in the Mariana Islands, passing by the busiest way station in the Pacific Ocean on this date, June 7, 1945. Down below is the gourd-shaped island of Iwo Jima. The U.S. Marines paid a terrible price capturing this little piece of volcanic waste. 4,590 young Marines lost their lives there and another 15,954 were wounded. After the capture of the island, more than 2,000 B-29s made emergency landings there, either

damaged or running low in fuel. It became known as a safe haven for over 20,000 crew members in those B-29s. (J.B. HUDSON)

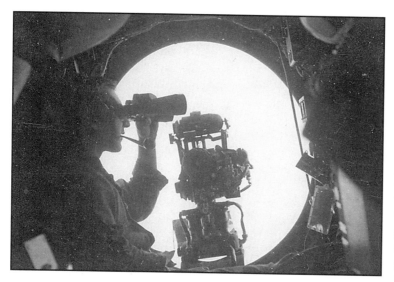

Jerry Benesh of the 6th Bomb Group, North Field, Tinian, sits in the right gunner's seat and calmly scans the skies with his binoculars for enemy fighters through the blister by his seat. Smoking pipes, as Jerry is doing, and cigarettes, were allowed in flight to and from the targets—that is, after the aircraft is safely off the ground, at cruising speed. The instrument in the center of the blister (white circle) is the remote controlled gunsight. With this sight, the gunner could fire .50-caliber machine guns in turrets several feet from him. (J.B. HUDSON)

This photo was taken from the nose of a B-29 just before dropping a load of supplies, including food, medicine, etc., in a POW camp just ahead. The camp was located in China, and held American and Allied troops. Because the Japanese were reluctant in giving locations of where the POW camps were located it was very difficult to find them, especially in China and Korea. (J.B. HUDSON)

Crew number 3909 of *Reamatroid*, 6th bomb Group, Tinian before entering plane for a mission to Japan. Kneeling, from left, Ed Russell, A/C; J.K. Anderson, pilot; Don Kearney, navigator; Charlie Hall, bombardier. Standing, from left, Joe Hudson, radar operator; Adrian Bee, gunner; John Heuer, CFC gunner; Ed Allgor, gunner; Bill Doland, flight engineer; Bill Jefferson, radio operator; and Don Gleacher, tail gunner. (Warren Higgins, later pilot, not pictured). (J.B. HUDSON)

B-29 PHOTO COMBAT DIARY

Close formation over Georgia. These two B-29 Superforts were built at the Bell plant at Marietta, Georgia, giving a close-up view of the smooth-skinned, streamlined heavy bomber. Marietta was one of four plants that produced Boeing Superforts during WWII. The other four were Boeing, Seattle; Benton, Wichita; and Martin, Omaha. Together, they produced 3,965 B-29s before the war ended. (PRESCOTT)

This photo of Captain Elbert L. Moore's B-29 crew was taken at Clovis Army Air Field, Clovis, New Mexico, by the nose of *Miss Carriage*, a B-29 used in training of Superfort crews. Front row, from left, Sgt. Robert M. Painter, radio; Cpl. Thaddeus E. Jedziniak, tail gunner; Cpl. Albert C. Furtney, right gunner; Sgt. Gerry T. Warren, CFC gunner; and Sgt. Norman F. Gunn, left gunner. Standing, from left, 1st Lt. Daniel R. Mickey, radar; Captain Elbert L. Moore, airplane commander; 2nd Lt. Wallace L. Page, flight engineer, (killed while flying in reserves at WWII), 1st Lt. Joseph G. Prescott, pilot; 2nd Lt. Gordon H. Woodward, navigator; and 1st Lt. James Fred Boone, bombardier. (PRESCOTT)

Diamond B, #9, is undergoing regular routine inspection as she sits on her hardstand in the 16th Bomb Group's area with the 315th Bomb Wing at Northwest Field, Guam. The picture was taken from the side door of another B-29 in a hardstand next to # 9. The ladder was used to board the Super-

forts in the gunners' pressurized section to the rear of the bomb bays. (HAROLD G. ALFORD)

This was the U.S. Army 2nd Repair Unit B-29 scrap yard on Iwo Jima. The repair unit had a ship anchored off shore that could build parts from scratch to repair damaged B-29s that landed there from missions over Japan. Aboard the ship also were two of the first five helicopters built for the Army abroad and could fly the parts to airstrips when completed, rather than transport them by boat. (HAROLD G. ALFORD)

Admiral Chester Nimitz, right, decorates Brigadier General "Rosey" O'Donnel, Commanding Officer of the 73rd Wing at Saipan, with a medal. Admiral Ninitz commanded the Pacific Navy Fleets during the march from Guadalcanal through the Middle Pacific to the Mariana Islands, where the B-29's 20th Air Force units began and finished the final assault on the Japanese homelands. (HAROLD G. ALFORD)

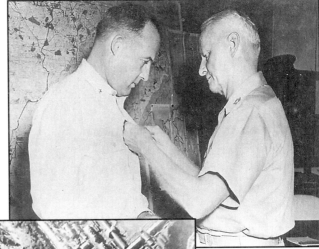

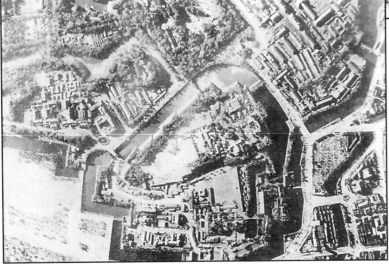

The Emperors Palace is shown in this ariel photo from about 30,000 feet altitude. A moat surrounds the palace itself as well as the entire complex of houses, needed for the household staff and advisors. It is located in mid-town Tokyo. (3RD PHOTO)

B-29 PHOTO COMBAT DIARY

This is a radar photograph showing target area after turning east following the first raid on Tokyo, March 9/10, 1945. Tokyo Bay is the dark area in the upper left. The three fingered lake northeast of Tokyo is shown in lower right. The bright dot south of, and below, the aircraft location is Chosi Point along Eastern shore of Honshu Island. (J.B. HUDSON)

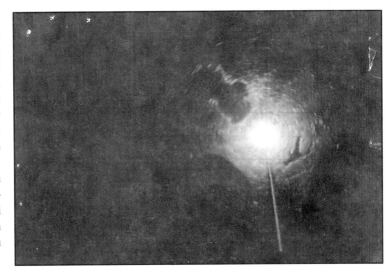

These repaired R-3350, 2200 horsepower radial engines, await their turn to be moved over to the repair area where the B-29s in the background need engine changes. B-29s from Guam, Tinian and Saipan all received repairs from the Army 2nd Repair Unit, as well as from a group of twenty trained mechanics and specialists who were sent to Iwo Jima from various Squadrons to do maintenance work on Iwo, when the bombing raids increased in size. (HAROLD G. ALFORD)

Work on the "line" is never done. Here a driver on a "tug" backs a Superfort into its hardstand, where it can be serviced before the next raid. Each B-29 had its own hardstand "resting place" near the landing strips at each of the bases in the Marianas. This group of B-29s were with the 16th Bomb Group, 315th Wing, at Northwest Field, Guam. (HAROLD G. ALFORD)

Jus' One Mo' Time was a 501st Bomb Group, 315th Wing, B-29B. It was produced by Bell at its Marietta, Georgia plant with its APG-17 radar unit called "Eagle" because supposedly the sharpness, like an eagle's eye, could pick out buildings in a target area at night with its advance radar. Nose art, girlie pictures and all, stayed on the 315th planes until the end of the war, unlike those with the 73rd. All girlie nose art was replaced there with a winged ball and spear insignia. (EVANS)

Salome, Where She Danced, serial #44-83892, 355th Squadron, 331st Bomb Group at Northwest Field, Tinian, was engaged in the strangest, but successful, mission a B-29 of WWII ever undertook. When the war ended, Colonel Willard W. Wilson, Squadron CO. , and his brother, Colonel Albert T. Wilson, Jr. , got permission to fly this plane to Mukden, in northern Manchuria to pick up their father, Colonel Albert T. Wilson, Sr., who was a POW since the Philippines fell early in the war, and was being held there by the Japanese. The name of the plane was changed to *Dode*, their father's nickname. A large pipe was printed on the nose because their Dad usually smoked a pipe. Clarence Juett, flight line chief, acted as crew chief on the flight which took three weeks to make, under most unusual conditions. (EVANS)

Using full flaps this 315th Wing B-29B is about to touch down at Northwest Field, at Guam

after a daylight mission to Japan. Other B-29s in the area, (upper right) are getting into position to enter the traffic pattern. One can be seen as a small speck on the horizon about to enter the traffic pattern. Crews always returned from targets in Japan individually (not in formation) in order to preserve gas on the return trip. (HAROLD G. ALFORD)

An ordnance man sits astride a 500-pound cluster bomb of incendiaries ready to be loaded into Z 24 of the 500th Bomb Group, 73rd Wing, at Saipan. Z 24, with the black stripe on lower part of vertical stabilizer, carried the name of *Pride of the Yankees*, which turned out to be somewhat of a

"hard-luck plane." Twice, during the war, the *Pride* had to return from missions to Japan on two engines, one of the very few B-29s to successfully accomplish that feat. (WES PALSEY)

The 497th Group's *Peace on Earth* was ditched by A/C Lieutenant Norman Westervelt on the way back from a mission to Tokyo on March 4, 1945. Nine men of the crew were rescued by a Dumbo amphibian. One of the crewman was never seen after the ditching, and Westervelt was washed off the wing as he tried to reach safety, and was never seen again. (HASSELL)

The 73rd Wing at Saipan lost lots of the earlier B-29s because of mechanical troubles, by enemy action over the target, or running short of fuel on the way back to home base. But not all of the Wing's Superforts were doomed to short lives. *For-*

bidden Fruit, shown here as maintenance men prepare the plane for another mission, eventually completed sixty-five missions against Japan before being sent home. (HASSELL)

WORLD WAR II

It made no difference whether the B-29 Superfortresses served in the CBI Theater, or the Mariana Islands in the Pacific, nose art ranged along about the same line. The crews liked for their airplane to have a pretty girl, mostly. The use of Lady was commonly seen and the Vegas type girl was usually thinly-clad. Crews in the 444th Bomb Group especially liked the word "Lady" associated with their aircraft name: There was *Lucky Lady*, *Lady in Waiting*, *Lady Frances*, *Lady Marge*, *Dragon Lady*, above, just to name a few. (EVANS)

Not all B-29 crews stayed with the "Lady" line. There were many "Gals" in names boldly stroked across the noses of some the the Superforts. Pictured is a name that strayed off toward a Disney character. Regardless of what the title may have been, the nose artists around the bases could come up with a good picture— as with this *Ghastly Goose* that flew with the 397th Bomb Group. (HASSELL)

Tail section of this Superfortress gets a going-over. At left, men remove the twin .50-caliber machine guns from the tail gunner's position for a clean up before an inspection. The gunner had a clear vision on three sides of the aircraft. He sat in the small pressurized compartment where the windows are located. The two men standing on the horizontal stabilizer pose for this picture after checking out other sections of the vertical stabilizer. V Square 9 was assigned to the 499th Bomb Group at Saipan. The man with his hand on the Square is Emil Goyich. (GOYICH)

The *Enola Gay* B-29 Superfortress, with Colonel Paul W. Tibbets, Jr., Commanding Officer of the 509th Composite Group, at the controls, is shown just seconds before touchdown at North Field, Tinian after a flight to Hiroshima, Japan that changed the course of history. The Hiroshima mission

was accomplished August 6, 1945, without a hitch. The weapon was "Little Boy" bomb, Uranium-235 core with gun mechanism. Participating in the mission were six other B-29s from the 509th Composite Group. These planes carried no bombs. They were used for blast measurement, photography and advance weather recon at Hiroshima, the primary target; Kokura, the secondary target; Nagasaki the tertiary target; and one plane as backup for *Enola Gay*, at Iwo Jima. (THOMAS COSTA)

Bud Sprenger, a Marine in the 3rd Battalion, 10th Marines, padded his take-home pay with artwork like the job he did on Captain Pershing Yon's *Coral Queen* in the 497th Bomb Group, Saipan. Sprenger decorated several B-29s of the 73rd Wing with nose art like *Coral Queen*, *Joker's Wild*, and others. His going price was about $175 plus a bottle or two of whisky for each job. (EVANS)

Lucky Lady, another of the "Lady" series of names from the 444th Bomb Group in the 58th Wing. When this photo was taken at Dudkhundi, this "Lady" had made fourteen regular missions and had made ten "Hump" supply trips to Kwanghan, China, the Group's forward base. (EVANS)

These three ordnance men are trying to send a message to "Tojo" and the Japanese people as they pose by a big five hundred pound demolition bomb. Before loading this one into the bomb bay of the awaiting Superfort, they painted this message on the bomb: "To Tojo—with regards—From the Goyich and Rudo families." (GOYICH)

The man on the mechanic's stand seems to be ready to begin painting some nose art on the nose of the Superfortress in the 16th Bomb Group, 315th Wing at Guam. Don't be fooled by the "finished" art work already applied to the nose of the aircraft. This piece of work was done fifty years after the man on the stand did his thing.

You'll note it is an official symbol of Boeing Airplane Company's 50th Anniversary of the first flight of the first B-29 built which took place in September, 1942 with test pilot Eddie Allen at the controls. Boeing invited all veterans of the old 20th Air Force to their 50th Anniversary celebration at their plant in Seattle in August, 1992. It took special knowledge in photography to "superimpose" the emblem on the nose of the airplane. Ed Hering, who was stationed on Guam in 1945 with the 16th Bomb Group, has that knowledge. (ED HERING)

Foremost in the minds of Allied leaders after the Peace Treaty was signed, was to try to locate all the Prisoner of War camps in Japan proper and elsewhere. B-29 crews were sent on search missions throughout Japan and as far away as China, Manchuria and Korea, in strong efforts to locate the POWs. It was urgent to find them as soon as possible, knowing that they would be possibly without food, medicine and other supplies. As soon as camps were located, it was decided to fly the supplies from Saipan, and consequently all planes participating in the "mercy missions" would be brought to Isley Field on Saipan to be loaded. This photo shows the seemingly endless rows of Superforts parked awaiting their turn to be loaded and to go on a real "peacetime" trip to Japan. (U.S. AIR FORCE PHOTO)

While the surrender ceremony was taking place on the *Missouri*, over 500 B-29 Superfortresses in a "Show of Power" fly over with every Group of the five Wings of B-29s that were so successful in forcing Japan to capitulate. They filled the skies over the area. In addition, Navy and Marine aircraft also took part in the giant

demonstration. Shown here are Superforts from the 40th Bomb Group in flight over the Battleship *Missouri* in Tokyo Bay during the signing of the Peace Treaty. (HARRY M. CHANGNON)

With the dropping of the atomic bombs on Hiroshima and Nigasaki, August 6th, and 9th, and after Emperor Hirohito overruled his military leaders to end the war August 15, 1945, Japanese surrender envoys were sent to General MacArthur's headquarters in the Phillipines, to make arrangements for a surrender ceremony to be held on the USS Battleship *Missouri* September 2, 1945. The envoys,

flying in a "Betty" bomber, painted white with a large black cross painted on the fuselage, stopped at an airfield at Ie Shima for refueling en route to Manila to meet General MacArthur. Guards were posted around the plane during the stop over. Ie Shima is the little island in the Ryukyus chain near Okinawa, where famed war correspondent Ernie Pyle was killed by a sniper's bullet. The fuel stop over at Ie Shima took place August 19, 1945. (RICHARD WOOD)

The above Superfort with the 20th Air Force insignia and the number 3 painted on it was one of the three B-29Bs getting finishing touches for a three ship nonstop record breaking flight from Japan to Washington. Brig. General Emmett "Rosey" O'Donnell, Commander of the 73rd Bomb Wing at Saipan from the beginning of the B-29 operation November 24, 1944 against Japan's home islands until the end of the war, would be the Airplane Commander of #3 on the flight. Flight Officer Charles R. Major would be a flight engineer on the aircraft. (ED HERING)

This load of supplies has just been released from the bomb bays of a 16th Bomb Group, 315th Bomb Wing Superfort. The picture was taken from the tail gunner's position and the POW camp has not come into view at the bottom of the picture. This camp was also located in northern Honshu. (ED HERING)

This photo of a POW camp in Japan was taken by a 73rd Wing crew member. You can see the POWs gathered outside in the street at lower left, below the PW sign. Prisoner of War camps were eventually found in Japan, China, Manchuria and Korea. The last supply drop by the Superfortresses was made on September 20, 1945. By that time 1,066 B-29s had participated in 900 effective missions to 154 camps. An estimated 63,500 Allied prisoners were provided 4,470 tons of supplies. During the "Missions of Mercy," eight B-29s were lost with seventy-seven crew members aboard. (73RD WING PHOTO)

Three Superforts stand ready to begin a 6,000 mile nonstop trip from Japan to Washington, D. C. One of the planes that will make the trip is not shown above. Not yet lined up at North Field, Guam September 16, 1945, is #2. Major General Curtis LeMay, Chief of Staff of the Strategic

Air Forces was the Airplane Commander of #2 on the record breaking flight. Lt. Gen. Barney M. Giles, deputy chief of U.S. Strategic Air Forces in the Pacific, commanded #1, and Brig. Gen. Emmett O'Donnell, commander of the 73rd Bomb Wing, commanded #3. General Jimmy Doolittle, not participating in the record setting flight, was commander of a fourth B-29 which acted as the baggage plane. From Guam, all four planes flew to Chitose Field, near Sapporo on Hokkaido, Japan's northernmost island. They left Chitose Field September 19, for Washington beginning at 4:01 PM with Gen. Giles leading in #1. Following was Gen. LeMay at 4:08, and Gen. O'Donnel at 4:15. Bad weather, including unexpected headwinds, forced the planes to land in Chicago for more fuel, after which they took off for Washington. The 80-piece Army Air Forces Band and a large delegation of dignitaries headed by Gen. Henry H. Arnold, Army Air Force Commander, were on hand to extend a big welcome. (ED HERING)

This camp was known as the UBE North POW camp. Located in north Honshu, it was one of the largest of the Allied internment compounds. Note signs that point to drop zones outside the rows of buildings. There were no open areas and falling drums would have certainly injured some of the men if dropped among the buildings.

Ed Hering, who was an armorer with the 501st Bomb Group, 315th Wing at Northwest Field on Guam, was another expert photographer, part time, during his World War II duty at Guam. His part time job and interest in photography, turned into a lifetime hobby and a full time photo service company. This photo of *Pom Pom* decorated with a thinly clad beauty is among his collection. (ED HERING)

This shoulder patch was adopted by the 20th Air Force soon after the newly organized unit became official on April 10, 1944. Under a plan agreed upon by Joint Chiefs of Staff ,the Twentieth was designated as a strategic Army Air Force, operating directly under the Joint Chiefs with General Hap Arnold as Commanding General. He acted as Army Air Forces executive agent to implement their directives. This was the first unit ever organized in any of the services specifically for a single type of weapon. The Twentieth's weapon was the B-29 Superfortress. (MARSHALL)

Newspaper headlines across the country blazed the news of the tremendous success the B-29s were having in bringing Japan closer to the surrender table as the spring of 1945 eased toward summer when the final blows were struck. The above accumulation of headlines tell the stories of the big fire raids and the successful aerial mining missions which blocked most ports around Japan. (MARSHALL)

This cartoon character duck painted on this 501st Bomb Group Superfort at Guam with the unusual name of *My Naked-* looks as if he had just jumped off of the funny pages. The worried look on his face projects a nervous situation because he probably pulled the ripcord too soon. The parachute is already open. Bomb emblems on the aircraft indicates it has completed eleven missions to targets in Japan. (ED HERING)

North Field open air theatre was located on the northern tip of Tinian. In the background three miles across a channel the island of Saipan can be seen. Of all the Mariana Islands, Saipan had the highest "mountains." Isley Field on Saipan was on the southern end of the island and the 73rd Wing was based there. It was from Isley Field that the 73rd Wing, first of the five Wings of 20th Air Force, was to begin operations from the Marianas, launching the first B-29 raid on Tokyo on November 24, 1944, with a 110 plane strike force. Ninety-nine Superforts made it to Japan, and only two B-29s were lost. (CARL GARNER)

Waddy's Wagon sported another piece of creative nose art. Portraying images of the whole flight crew, with captain Waddy out front, it came to Saipan with the 497th Bomb Group, and began participating in bombing missions with the original crews of the 73rd Wing, the first Wing to begin operations from the Mariana Islands, in November, 1945. The entire crew and the *Wagon* were lost in one of the earlier missions against targets in Japan. (RUST)

Lieutenant Litchfield, and crew, pose for this picture in 1945 at North Field, on Tinian. They have their Mae West life jackets on and are about to enter their plane for a mission to a target in Japan. The one-eyed Pirate symbol painted on their plane means they were with the 6th Bomb Group, 313th Wing, which was the second Wing to reach the Mariana Islands to begin the final aerial assault against Japan. The crew and Group received the OTU (combat) training at Grand Island Army Air Field, and departed for overseas in November 1944, in three echelons. The ground echelon left the 18th of November, the second left on the 29th of November, and the air echelon and key ground personal, mechanics, etc., started the overseas flights in January, and continued until January 26, 1945, when the last plane arrived on Tinian. Col. Kenneth H. "Hoot" Gibson was the CO of the 6th Bomb Group. (MATTHEW HEGERLE)

Colonel "Pappy" Haynes and his *Thumper* crew: Left to right, standing: Lt. Mullens, Lt. Bogan, Col. Haynes, Lt. Phelps and Capt. Smith; Kneeling, left to right: Sgt. Guillen, Sgt. Penrod, Sgt. Alleman, Sgt. Monroe, Sgt. Newton and Sgt. Migliaccio. (TONY MIGLIACCIO)

The Lake Weeks crew at Saipan. They flew with the 878th Squadron, 499th Bomb Group. Standing, left to right: Lake Weeks, airplane commander; Eugene F. Parrish, pilot; Robert P. Green, navigator; Leslie Culbrandson, bombardier; Landon H. Cullu, engineer. Front row: George Beaudry, David L. Megchelsen, James J. Trevor, John E. Elrey, Burdell C. Hanson and Clyde N. Respass. (MARSHALL)

B-29 PHOTO COMBAT DIARY

This photo shows a busy railway yard located in downtown Tokyo, and was made by the 3rd Photo Recon Squadron before the fire raids devastated the area. (SPIETH)

Major David J. Liebman's crew, with the 878th Bomb Squadron, 499th Bomb Group at Saipan. They were among the original flight crews to arrive at Saipan, but by the time they completed their combat tour, just before the end of hostilities, they had to fly the increased number of missions (35). From left, standing: Liebman, airplane commander; Herbert L. Kelley, pilot; John E. Kuchenbecker, engineer; Leo E. Tippe, navigator; Harold D. Mays, bombardier; Lewis L. Walthour,

CFC gunner; Front row: Robert D. Doty, radar; Theo D. Sims, radio; Joseph T. Mora, left gunner; Dominick Parrone, right gunner; Odell James, tail gunner. (MARSHALL)

Skimming the tops of cumulus clouds, the B-29s from the 9th Bomb Group, 313th Wing, Tinian, hustle towards targets in Japan's home islands. These clouds were not too troublesome, but when big weather fronts built up between Iwo Jima and Japan, that was a different problem. (DOTY)

The John Handwerker crew, of the 93rd Bomb Group, 314th Wing on Guam, pose by *City of Memphis*. Standing, left to right: Bernard Sisman, navigator; Charles Boothby, pilot; Handwerker, Airplane Commander; Frankland W. McDonald, instrument specialist; Wilbur Davis, Jr., bombardier. Kneeling: Joseph C. Kordella, tail gunner; John F. Ladick, right gunner; Donald D. Simpson, CFC gunner; Ernest C. Kramer, left gunner; and Albert E. Hill, flight engineer. (HANDWERKER)

Fever From the South was one of the early B-29s to arrive at Saipan with the 500th Bomb Group, 73rd Wing, based at Isley Field. When this photo was snapped, she had made only three missions to Japan, one of which was the first B-29 raid on Tokyo, November 24, 1944. That raid was a daylight mission and altitudes ranged from 27-32,000 feet. (HASSELL)

Cutting it close—Captain William R. Howard, standing, left, and his crew, ran out of fuel just as they reached their forward base at Heinching, China, returning from the October 25, 1944, raid on the Omura Aircraft plant on the Japanese home island of Kyushu. The crew was attached to the  40th Bomb Group, 58th Wing, XX Bomber Command, stationed at Chakulia, India. It was the Group's Mission #13. Luckily no one was injured in the near mishap. (WM. R. HOWARD)

The crew of *Shag'n Home* pose by the nose for a picture at their base at West Field on Tinian. The nose symbols indicate the crew had been credited with three Japanese fighter kills, and 2½ "Hump" missions over the Himalayan mountains. Left to right, standing: Harry M. Changnon, copilot on crew; Duncan; Smith; Redgate; Bryant. Kneeling: McArdle; Murray; Nickerson; Healey; Terry and Page. (CHANGNON)

Ken Dothage poses with both his flight and ground crew beside the *Honey Bell Honey*. Standing, from left to right: John Laxton, Eric Buzza, Joseph Valley, Ken Dothage and Pat Dalay. Middle row: George Ahern, Clyde Beckley, Conrad Becker, Harry Pudlofsky and Harvey Chelf. The maintenance crew, front row, are unidentified. The veteran *Honey* shows she had marked up forty bombing missions, six "Hump" utility missions, and the crew had shot down two Japanese fighters when this photo was made in the 40th Bob Group on Tinian. (E. BUZZA)

Indian women haul gravel and building material in baskets balanced on top of their heads. Their work was instrumental in building hardstands for the B-29s and buildings needed at air-bases in India. (CHANGNON)

This B-29 crew's picture was taken in front of a B-17. The reason it was not snapped by a shining new Superfortress, was most of the combat training, before departing for India, had to be done in old B-17s. Modifications slowed delivery of the B-29s, especially to the 58th and 73rd Wings for training. (PERRY/CHANGNON)

Crew of the *Tokyo Rose*, first B-29 to fly over Tokyo. Commanded by Captain Ralph Steakly of 3rd Photo Recon Squadron, the historical flight took place November 1, 1944. Luckily,

weather was clear in the Tokyo area, and the crew was able to get excellent pictures to help establish targets for future bombing missions. Left to right during the decoration ceremonies for each crew member: S/Sgt. William O. Starks, S/Sgt. William J. Arnett, S/Sgt. Harley W. Clark, Sgt. Walter C. Marvin, T/Sgt. Marcus M. Johnson, T/Sgt. Fred H. Hutchins, Sgt. Harold L. McCommon, Lt. Charles G. Hart, Lt. John R. Burke, Lt. Claude Stambaugh and Capt. Ralph D. Steakley. (U.S. AIR FORCE PHOTO)

B-29 PHOTO COMBAT DIARY

Lady in Waiting, serial number 44-84068, was a latecomer to the 462nd Bomb Group, 58th Wing, at West Field, Tinian. A replacement crew brought *Lady* direct from the States after the India based 58th Wing had moved to West Field on Tinian. The 462nd Group, along with other Groups of the 58th Wing, made its first strike from Tinian on May 5, 1945. They accompanied the 73rd Wing in a 170 plane mission to Hiro, on the main island of Honshu, and hit an airplane industrial section of the city. (EVANS)

This is how supplies for prisoners of war looked as they drifted down into the compound from the bomb bays of the Superforts. The POWs were not long in establishing drop zones in the compounds and plainly marking the safe places to make drops. The much needed food, clothing and medicines did not always land in the marked drop zones, however. In some instances, the heavy 55 gallon drums struck buildings, knocking huge holes in them. And the missions were not always "milk runs." This was a "mercy mission" to a camp in Japan and on one such mission, Jack Riggs and crew of the 40th Bomb Group, were killed. They crashed and all crew members lost their lives on August 30, 1945. (SKAER/CHANGNON)

Captain Les Hodson, standing left, and crew, completed 35 missions with the 878th Squadron, 499th Bomb Group at Saipan. Standing left to right: Hodson, airplane commander; Leonard Shelton, pilot; Robert Stack, bombardier; Niles Larsen, navigator; Fred Matthews, engineer. Front row: Milton Kornman, George Fuller, Elmer Blackmer, Jr., Alex L. Toyzon, Jr., Thomas Armitage and William J. Murray. (MARSHALL)

General view of 73rd Bomb Wing Headquarters Section on Saipan in November, 1944. The wooden building to the right, would be the officers mess hall, not yet completed when this photo was taken. (U.S. AIR FORCE PHOTO)

This photo of snow capped Mount Fuji, Japan's tallest mountain, was taken from the right blister of a Superfortress. (CHANGNON)

This is a photo of the notorious Kempei Tai police and military prison located near the Imperial Palace in downtown Tokyo. Hundreds of downed B-29 crewmen were incarcerated here in what was to be known as horsestalls in the one story building, front, once used as horse stables. Some were held in solitary confinement, forbidden to speak to anyone, unless spoken to, and then only by a guard. Besides being forced to live on starvation rations, most American POWS were beaten unmercifully. (SCOT DOWNING)

B-29 PHOTO COMBAT DIARY

The harbor at Tinian was not as deep, or as suitable, as were those at Guam and Saipan. However, smaller ships, like the supply ships above, made it in pretty close to shore. During the invasion of Iwa Jima, the harbor at Saipan was jammed with ships as far out as eight miles from shore. (H. WILLIS)

This picture of Bob Winters and crew by *Hump-Happy Pappy* was taken in India before the Group, along with the entire 58th Wing, moved to Tinian in the Pacific. (CHANGNON)

Captain Merle Skousen, center, front, with his crew, with the 25th Squadron, 40th Bomb Group, pose in front of their B-29 at Chakulia, India, early in 1945. (CHANGNON)

General view of the 881st Squadron area of the 500th Bomb Group, Saipan, in the Mariana Islands. The 73rd Wing at Isley Field on Saipan with its four Groups, the 497th, 498th, 499th and 500th, was the first Wing of the 21st Bomber Command, 20th Air Force, to begin bombing the main island of Honshu on November 24, 1944. (U.S. Air Force Photo)

The Red Cross Hospitality Shack on Tinian: 1945. One of the two most popular gathering spots on the islands for the returning combat crews from a mission. The Red Cross girls gave out coffee and doughnuts along with back home smiles. For most, however, the whiskey shot shack, run by a hard nose flight surgeon, was available just outside the briefing and interrogation hut, for ONE 2-ounce shot of whiskey, supposedly to settle your nerves after a long flight. If

you got to know the flight surgeon or his helpers well enough, you could scrounge at least two or maybe three shots for relaxation sake. (CHANGNON)

Major General Emmett O'Donnel conversing with two of his staff officers in front of his 73rd Bomb Wing Headquarters on Saipan in December, 1944. (U.S. Air Force Photo)

Construction of North Field on Tinian, on a twenty-four hour, seven day a week schedule, by the 67th Seabee Battalion, with bulldozers, trucks and crushed coral rock, was ready to receive the 313th Wing on its four hugh parallel runways by December, 1944. First to arrive was the 504th Group, followed by the 505th, the 6th and 9th Groups. Activity during the construction at the north end of Tinian is demonstrated by picture above. (ED HERING)

Airplane mechanics with a new type engine hoist in place at 40th Bomb Group Air Base at Piardoba, India, prepare to change an engine on the Superfort. (CHANGNON)

Memphis Maid with 14 missions to Japan rest in hard stand at Saipan, with the 498th Bomb Group, 73rd Wing. (MILLER)

These happy warriors wave to friends in the plane taxiing out for another mission. The hand wavers were with Captain Sy Sylvester's crew. One reason they were so happy, they had completed their combat tour of 35 missions. Left to right: Butscher, Brown, Yensen and Foley. (SYLVESTER)

The not-so-happy looking warriors may relax a bit after getting used to rolling with the waves in a Navy troopship that is taking them homeward after the battles. Adrian Bee and Joe Hudson, seated, with other members of the 39th Squadron, 6th bomb Group, ordered to take the *Winged Arrow* troopship back to the West Coast, after hostilities had ended. When the war ended, B-29 crews from the

39th Bomb Squadron had completed a total of 79 combat missions against targets in Japan, flying from North Field, Tinian. Thirteen Japanese fighters were shot down during these missions. (HUDSON)

August 15, 1945 was a happy day for these men celebrating the end of the war at an officer's club on Saipan. This celebration was called the General "Rosey" O'Donnell VJ Day Party. Some of these men had been on the island since October, 1944, soon after Saipan was captured from the Japanese, and runways were ready to accept the B-29 Superfortresses. (HREN)

B-29 PHOTO COMBAT DIARY

Lady Marge was a record breaking B-29 pioneer that survived 37 bombing missions against Japanese targets, plus 22 "Hump" supply runs over the Himalayan Mountains before setting a world speed record on her homeward bound leg from Honolulu to Washington, D. C. September 1, 1945. *Lady* was assigned to Commander Al Harvey's 444th Bombardment Group (VH), 67th Squadron of the 58th Bomb Wing. The 58th Wing (20th Bomber Command) was the first B-29 Superfortress unit to be assigned combat duty against Japan. The four Groups of the 58th were deployed to bases in India and their first mission against a Japanese target was to Bangkok's railway yards June 5, 1944. When the Wing moved lock, stock and barrel from India and China to West Field at Tinian, *Lady Marge* was ready for more combat missions to the home islands of Japan. On September 1, 1945, one day before the "peace signing" in Tokyo Bay, officially ending World War II, the veteran Superfort showed she still had plenty of spunk left. She broke a world record of speed and distance by flying from Honolulu to Washington, D.C., averaging 285 miles per hour. (MANN/SCHIRMER COLLECTION)

The first B-29 to reach the Pacific was *Joltin' Josie, The Pacific Pioneer*. Brig. General Haywood Hansell, Commander of the XXI Bomber Command, was at the controls with Major Jack Catton, the regular airplane commander of the plane in the right seat, arriving at Isley Field October 12, 1944. Upon departing from the plane, the General greeted the large crowd of ground personnel, Seabees, engineers and Navy personnel with this statement: "When we do a little fighting we will do some more talking!" Major Catton, now deceased, remained in service after WWII and eventually reached the rank of four-star General. The 73rd Bomb Wing (VH), with its four Groups, would follow soon. (RUST)

Dauntless Dotty led a 110 plane daylight high altitude strike against a target in Tokyo November 24, 1944. It was the first B-29 mission against Tokyo since the Doolittle surprise attack launched from aircraft carrier, USS *Hornet*, April 18, 1942. Brig. General Emmett O'Donnell, 73rd Wing Commander, was at the controls of the lead aircraft, along with Col. Robert Morgan, a Squadron CO in the 497th Bomb Group on Isley Field, Saipan. Col. Morgan can be remembered as the Pilot of the famous *Memphis Belle*, the first B-17 to complete 25 missions in Europe and return to the U.S. (C. SNOW)

Some Punkins, #84, serial number 44-27296, was delivered to the 509th Composite Group, Wendover AAF, UT, and assigned to Crew B-7, Captain James P. Price Jr. A/C in April, 1945. Other flight crew members were Bednorez, P; Collinson, Nav.; Costa Bomb.; Adkins, FE; Byrd, Radio; Joe Brown, Radar; Bysom TG, and Fred Brown, Scan/Asst. FE. Ground crew included: Carrigon, Myers, Compronio, Crotty, Madrid, Josefiak and Miller. The crew participated in five regular combat "Pumpkin" mis-

sions, after arriving at North Field, Tinian where the 509th Composite Group and supporting units were based. After hostilities ceased *Punkins* returned to Roswell AAF, NM, in November, 1945. In March 1946 the aircraft participated in Task Force 1.5 (Operation Crossroads) at Bikini Atol. Dropped from inventory August, 1946, and scrapped. (CARL GARNER)

The nose artist in the 501st Bomb Group, 315th Wing at Guam went all out with this rendition of *Ten Knights in a Bar Room*. The crew of the B-29B Superfort must have been a happy-go-lucky bunch, especially after a few shots of spirits. The 315th Wing based at Northwest Field was the last of five B-29 Wings to reach the Mariana Islands. Modified to eliminate all gun turrets except the tail gun position, the four Groups of the Wing were instrumental in weakening the enemy's abili-

ty to resist the Superforts' all out assault, as the war moved toward its final phase. With a new radar system called the "Eagle," they could pinpoint oil refineries and storage areas, and by the time the war ended they had destroyed most of Japan's refineries. (ED HERING)

Mention the name *Enola Gay* and most people will recognize the name as that of the B-29 Superfortress that dropped the atomic bomb on Hiroshima, the first of the two atomic bombs dropped against Japanese cities. With Colonel Paul W. Tibbets, Jr., CO of the 509th Composite Group, at the controls, the mission to Hiroshima August 6, 1945 was authorized by Field Order No. 13, Special Bombing Mission

No. 13, Operations Order No. 35 of the 509th Composite Group stationed at North Field, Tinian. The weapon was called "Little Boy" Bomb, Uranium-235 Core, with Gun Mechanism. This mission changed the world as we knew it, and with a second bomb on Nagasaki, forced Japan to capitulate, ending World War II. (CARL GARNER)

A lot of originality showed up in the names and artwork that graced the B-29s during the final assault on the Japanese home islands. Pictured on this Superfort in the 501st Bomb Group, 315th Wing at Guam is one that always brought chuckles from an observer. The *01' Matusalum* character with white hair and a long white beard is showing his age, but is up and at 'em and ready for another mission to Japan. (ED HERING)

First to go over the century mark in missions to Korea. With 100 mission bomb emblems painted around the 19th bomb Group shield *Blue Tail Fly* displays how she made part of the famed Group's history. The 19th was almost wiped out when the Japanese attacked the Phillipines at the very beginning of World War II. A few of the B-17s of the 19th made it to Australia, and later the Group regrouped and became part of the 314th Bomb Wing at Guam and her B-29 crews during the final assault on Japan

were among the most decorated for valor in the 20th Air Force. When North Korea crossed the 38th parallel and attacked the South Koreans, the 22 plane 19th Bomb Group, again stationed at Guam, being the closest American bombers to the conflict, were ordered by General MacArthur, then UN Supreme Commander, into combat against North Korea. The Group was once again first to go into combat, still with their seven year-old Superforts. (GEORGE AMTHOR)

There was more than one *Thumper*, one of Disney's characters, gracing Superfortresses in the Marianas. This one was assigned to the 9th Bomb Group, 313th Wing at Tinian. Another was assigned to the 499th Bomb Group, 73rd Wing, Saipan, which was flown by Col. "Pappy" Haynes on several missions. He and his crew brought the veteran *Thumper* back to the States before hostilities ceased and they participated in a bond selling tour throughout the country. Most combat crews longed for a bond tour when they finished their missions, but only a few were so lucky. Col. Haynes had completed a tour in Europe and also in the Pacific. He was credited with bombing all three capital cities of the Axis: Berlin, Rome and Tokyo. (RUST)

Nose art junkies got an eyeful when *Sizzling Suzy* taxied by in the 501st Bomb Group, 315th Bomb wing at Northwest Field on Guam. Nose art aside, one can not help but notice the slim smooth line of a turretless fuselage of the B-29B the 315th Wing used. It was apparent before the 315th's four Groups were ready to head for the Marianas, the Japanese fighters had been deflated to almost no show of serious opposition to the Superforts. All 315th Wing B-29s were modified and turrets were eliminated. (ED HERING)

Up an' Atom, #88, serial number 44-27304, joined the 509th Composite Group at Wendover AAF, UT, in April, 1945 and was assigned to Crew B-10 with George W. Marquardt as airplane commander. In June they moved to North Field, Tinian. Other crew members: Anderson, Pilot; Gackenback, Nav.; Strudwick, Bomb.; Corlias, FE; Coble, Radio; DiJulio, Radar; Bierman, TG; and Capua, Asst. FE/Scan. Ground crew: Gulick, Brown, Huddleston, Hammons, Berzinis, Bezdegian and Mason. At Tinian, *Up an' Atom* completed four "Pumpkin" missions with regular Bomb Groups. August 9, 1945 the plane with A/C Marquardt at the controls flew a weather recon. mission to Kokura, in conjunction to the 2nd Atomic Mission to Nagasaki. The aircraft returned to Roswell, NM in November, 1945, and in April, 1946, participated in Task Force 1.5 (Operation Crossroads). After being assigned to several stations for various duties, it was eventually transferred to the Navy to be used as target practice by Navy planes at China Lake, California, and scrapped in 1956. (CARL GARNER)

Five hundred pound demolition bombs spew from these Big Z Superfortresses, letting everyone around them know that they are from the 500th Bomb Group, 73rd Wing from Saipan. When B-29s first started bombing targets in the Japanese home islands, all missions were high altitude daylight raids, mostly with  demolition or high explosive bombs. Early missions were flown at altitudes as high as thirty to thirty-two thousand feet. Later, when opposition diminished, altitudes were lowered to about 25,000 feet. When fighter protection came on line in April, 1945, daylight raids were lowered to as low as 15-18,000 feet. Night missions with incendiary bombs were dropped to a low of 5,000 feet. (CLAUDE LOGAN)

 Lined up on the parking area are three of the 15 B-29Bs modified to carry the atomic bombs. Only two of the fifteen dropped A-bombs on Japanese cities. All except one participated in at least four or five "Pumpkin" missions flying with other Groups of the B-29s on Guam, Tinian and Saipan, supposedly to get the feel of flying over Japan. The above planes had their 509th insignia painted on their vertical stabilizer when this picture was taken. When they participated in regular missions the arrow inside the big circle was changed to the Group they were flying with. This was done to prevent the Japanese from suspecting that a "new" Wing has arrived. From right to left, the Superforts above are *Enola Gay*, #82; *Full House*, # 83 and *Some Punkins*, #84. (CARL GARNER COLLECTION)

Big Stink, #90, serial number 44-27354, was delivered to the 509th Composite Group May 25, 1945, assigned to Crew C-12, Herman S. Zahn AC. Other flight crew members were: Dickman, Pilot; Deutch, Nav.; Ormond, Bomb.; Elder, FE; Bauer, Radio; Clapso, Radar; Allen, TG; and Corey Asst. FE/Scan. This crew flew no combat missions due to late arrival on Tinian. However, Classen, crew A-5, flew two "Pumpkin" missions in the plane, and McKnight and his B-8 crew was back up for 1st A-bomb mission (*Enola Gay*) standing by at Iwo Jima. The Hopkins crew C-14 used the plane on the 2nd Atomic mission as camera ship. The name was changed to *Dave's Dream* for Task Force 1.5 (Operation Crossroads), and dropped test "Fat Man" type bombs at Bikini. After several duty assignments, the plane was stored at Davis-Monthan AFB, Arizona, in June, 1959. It was then dropped from inventory and scrapped in February, 1960. (CARL GARNER)

Brig. General Paul W. Tibbets, Jr. (retired) former commander of the 509th Composite Group and airplane commander of *Enola Gay* on the 1st atomic bombing mission against Hiroshima, Japan, left, with Jack McGregor, former airplane commander in the 869th Squadron, 497th Bomb Group, at Saipan, during World War II. This photo was taken during a meeting at the Smithsonian Institute in 1988. McGregor was a docent at the Barber Facility, NA&SM at the Smithsonian at the time the two old friends met. General Tibbets was instrumental, along with thousands of veterans, especially Air Force people, in forcing a change in displaying the nose section of the *Enola Gay* at the institution during the 50th anniversary celebration of the end of World War II. (McGREGOR)

Rested up and ready for another night mission against fuel refineries or storages somewhere in Japan, this group of B-29 Superfortresses of the 501st Bomb Group, 315th Wing, at Northwest Field, Guam, are shown in the hardstands at the base. Like the other Groups of the 315th, the 501st planes were equipped with the "Eagle" radar system. Officially known as the AN/APQ/7 radar set, the system was capable of identifying a single building and was a great improvement over the older AN/APQ/13 system. (ED HERING)

Bockscar, #7, serial number 44-27297, was delivered to 509th Composite Group, and assigned to Crew C-13 with Captain Frederick C. Bock, airplane commander. The plane arrived at Wendover AAF, Utah, April, 1945, and to North Field, Tinian in June, 1945, and made three combat missions to Japan (Pumpkin) with Bock's crew C-13 on two missions and with Albury's C-15 on the other. Major Charles W. Sweeney, CO of 393rd Bomb Squadron, was A/C with the Albury Crew C-15, with Albury Pilot and Fred Olivi, Co-Pilot, took the

plane on the Nagasaki mission. *Bockscar* participated in the Task Force 1. 5 at Bikini in June, 1946. In September, 1946, it was dropped from inventory and transferred to the U.S. Air Force Museum at Wright-Patterson base, Dayton, Ohio, where it is on display. (CARL GARNER)

Necessary Evil, serial no. 44-86291, was delivered to 509th Composite Group, at Wendover AAF, Utah, in June, 1945, and assigned to Crew C-14. The aircraft made five "Pumpkin" missions to targets in Japan, and was the camera ship on the second atomic mission to Nagasaki. The aircraft participated in Task Force 1.5 (Operation Crossroads) and stayed on active duty until November, 1956. It was dropped from inventory and used for Navy target practice. (GARNER)

One of the most visited tourist spots at Tinian is this well-kept location of the atomic bomb pit number 1. This is where "Little Boy" atomic bomb was loaded into the bomb bays of "Enola Gay", the B-29 Superfortress that delivered the bomb on the first mission to Hiroshima. The bomb was so large, weighing in the neighborhood of 10,000 pounds, a pit had to be dug and the plane taxied over the spot where the bomb was lifted into the belly of the airplane. Many Japanese tourists visit the spot; as you can see, the message is in both English and Japanese. (GREG FIELD)

Tu Yung Tu with the 501st Bomb Group, 315th Wing, Northwest Field, Guam, carries its message loud and clear with a Chinese twang to it. There was an old saying during the World War II era that made the rounds, and nose art on the above black bottomed Superfort was derived probably from the saying; "Too Young To Cut The Mustard." (ED HERING)

Rosie Marie turned many an eye, whether in her hardstand in the 501st Bomb Group area at Guam, or taxiing out for a bombing mission to oil refineries in Japan. Folks back in the States got their first similar eyeview of nose art when B-29s from the 73rd Wing started returning to the States after finishing combat tours, or for crews to train for flight leader refresher courses. It wasn't long after that orders came down from 73rd Wing headquarters to replace all girlie nose art with a unified Wing Ball and Spear. The reason for the change being "boosting personnel morale" they said. (ED HERING)

The dedication of the B-29 Superfortress, below, to *Admiral Chester Nimitz* at Northwest Field on Guam, June 15, 1945, was the rankest ceremony ever performed in the Mariana Islands in WWII by far. The dedication of a Superfort to be named for Admiral Nimitz was the brainchild of General Armstrong, 315th Wing Commander for the Fleet Admiral's "marvelous logistic support he had given to the B-29s," according to Colonel (later Brig. Gen.) Boyd Hubbard, Jr. Commander of the 501st Bomb Group of the 315th. Col. Hubbard was put in charge of selecting the plane, which he did, and Adm. Nimitz sent his own painter to paint the aircraft with his name and five star flag. None other than five-star General of the Air Force Hap Arnold was on hand to make the presentation before a large assembly of officers and men of all Services. (ED HERING)

Some strange names showed up on some of the Superfortresses that roamed the skies over Japan. We never got the message the crew in the 498th Group, 73rd Wing at Saipan was trying to portray with this rendition of *Tanaka Termite*. The well-formed lassie in this nose art didn't resemble a termite to this observer. *Termite* was just getting her feet wet when this photo was made, showing only ten mission emblems at this juncture at Isley Field, Saipan. (RUST)

Operation officer in Jeep, lower right, checks with mechanic about the status of the flight lead Superfort sitting in the hardstand at North Field on Tinian. The big circle indicates the airplane is with the 9th Bomb Group, 313th Wing, the second B-29 Wing to begin operation against Japan's home islands from the Marianas. The black and gold stripes around the rear of the fuselage means the commander of the aircraft is a flight leader. The stripes made it easier to see and identify when planes in the Group were trying to rendezvous. (CURTIS)

This is an overview photo shot of the 6th Bomb Group, 313th Wing on Tinian, looking north. The "mountains" in the background are on Saipan, where the 73rd Wing was stationed, across a three mile wide channel. The Big Circle Wing included the 6th BG with the big R in the circle; the 9th BG had a big X in the circle; the 504th BG had a big E in the circle, and the 505th had a big W. (CARL GARNER)

Amateur photographers stationed in the tropic islands of the Pacific during World War II had to take extra precautions to protect their color film, because of the erratic weather and hot climate. Claude Logan, who was a 2nd Lt. Flight Engineer on the John Ryan crew in the 500th Bomb Group, 499th Group, 73rd Wing at Saipan, was very fortunate with his film and came home with some of the finest color slides of B-29s and views of Saipan and other Pacific Islands this observer has seen. Logan took the above shot of *Raunchy Rambler* which did its rambling with the 500th Group. (CLAUDE LOGAN)

This B-29 is one of the three Superforts used in the try for a record non-stop flight from Japan to Washington after the Japanese surrendered in 1945. Final adjustments and inspections were being made with weather shields above engines #3 and #4 to protect mechanics while working on engines. This aircraft is identified by the Twentieth Air Force patch

painted on the vertical stabilizer, along with a #1, indicating this plane was flown by Lt. Gen. Barney M. Giles, deputy chief of U.S. Strategic Air Forces in the Pacific, as the airplane commander on the try for a record flight. Major General Curtis LeMay was airplane commander on Superfort #2, and Brig. Gen. Emmett O'Donnell, 73rd Wing CO, was commander of #3. The flight had to land at Chicago, and refuel before flying on to Washington. (E.M. GILLUMZ)

The sign out front of this Superfort in the 499th Bomb Group at Saipan warned anyone entering the cockpit that bombs were loaded in the bomb bays. Flight crews always made preflight inspections, but the armorers always put out the sign as an extra precaution to help prevent an accident, such as pushing a button and releasing the bombs on the ground. (MARSHALL)

The Big Circle E and the red tip on top of the vertical stabilizer identified the aircraft as one from the 504th Bomb Group, 313th Wing on Tinian. The Group's area was near one of the four parallel runways on the world's largest airfield at the northern end of Tinian. When the 509th Composite

Group and its support units came to the Pacific to begin its atomic bombing missions against Japan, this special Group was assigned space near the above area. (CURTIS)

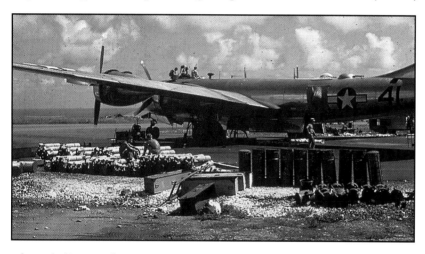

Much preparation went into getting the B-29s ready to go on a bombing mission. The mechanics, the armorers, and all hands, including the cooks and all of the other ground personnel, had a big hand in the overall operation, without whose dedication the mission could not have gotten off the ground. (CLAUDE LOGAN)

The crew of this unnamed B-29 Superfortress used a different angle in having their missions painted on its nose. A veteran of the 58th Bomb Wing in both the CBI and the Pacific Theatres, this crew marked up twenty-one bombing missions and eight "Hump" supply trips across the Himalayan Mountains while stationed in India and on Tinian Island. What makes this display different is the actual date each mission was flown is painted below every bomb emblem. (CURTIS)

This landing accident took place at Isley Field, Saipan, when a Superfort pancaked in. The pilot either had trouble stopping the plane due to brake failure, or he could have run completely out of fuel and had to belly land with wheels up. Only enough gas was loaded into the aircraft to make it to and from a target in Japan. If something happened to cause excess fuel consumption or flying off course, some of the B-29s just made it back to base, and in many instances, the crews had to ditch in the ocean. (WARREN THOMPSON)

Another creative piece of nose art is displayed on this B-29 from the 501st Bomb Group, 315th Wing at Northwest Field, Guam. *Jughound-Jelopy* artist portrays a theme of a faithful ole jughound rushing his very large jug of spirits to somewhere, possibly to his crew. This aircraft had its underside painted black, as did some of the Groups in the 315th Wing. Since most of the missions were made at night, the black belly helped prevent the ack ack boys on the ground from getting a gleaming clear shot at them. (ED HERING)

Superforts ready for a "Mercy Mission" to POW camps located throughout Japan and Asia locations. When the war ended and after POW camps were pinpointed where allied and Twentieth Air Force men were, B-29s from all Groups in the Marianas participated in delivering food, clothing, medicine and other supplies by air drops. The planes were all loaded at Isley Field where the above B-29s are lined up and ready to be loaded. (CURTIS)

Nipp On Ese made it back to North Field, Tinian, from a bombing mission to Japan, but judging by the shape the ship is in at the end of the runway, this may have been the final flight of the 313th Wing Superfort. Brakes evidently failed when the plane landed, possibly due

to ruptured hydraulic lines caused by anti-aircraft flak shrapnel over Japan. (CARL GARNER)

Million Dollar Baby II portrays a couple of interesting features in nose art paintings. First, and secondary to the features, the 468th aircraft shows proof that she had participated in 28 bombing missions when this photo was snapped, but the most interesting fact is the pair of silkless stockings covering her legs. Silk was short during WWII, and of course you can tell this was the era before the pantyhose. (WEBER)

This fifty mission veteran of World War II's 73rd Wing at Saipan is shown as she sat "mothballed" awaiting further call to service at Davis-Monathan Air Force Base at Tuscon, Ari-

zona, in 1946. Like hundreds of WWII B-29 Superforts, *Fever From The South* was returned to storage spots scattered mostly in the western states. You can tell the nose has been "cocooned" or mothballed. Some of the standing by B-29s were cleaned up and went off again to fight in the Korean War. (MANN/SCHIRMER COLLECTION)

There was a *Sentimental Journey* in almost every Group of B-29s in the Mariana Islands during World War II. This one flew with the 58th Wing, 444th BG, 678th Squadron, based at West Field, Tinian. Judging by the missions this aircraft made, it made it to the Marianas pretty late, and did not participate in missions from India. This *Sentimental Journey* was among the B-29s returning from the war mothballed at Davis-Monathan AFB, Tuscon. (MANN/SCHIRMER COLLECTION)

Miss Judy shows no mercy on the "Tojo" character, commonly known as the number one enemy by Twentieth Air Force folk in the Pacific during World War II. *Judy*, in this piece of creative nose art on a 462nd Bomb Group Superfort in the 58th Wing at West Field, Tinian, lowers on Tojo's head, and the stars are flying. (CURTIS)

This is how the B-29 Superforts looked lined up in perfect rows at Davis-Monathan Air Force Base in 1946 and 1947, before a decision was made as to what planes were to be mothballed for possible reactivation, or to be removed from the inventory and sent to a base for scrapping. Hundreds of the Superforts were scrapped and pots and pans were manufactured by companies that rushed to purchase the material. Some of these mothballed planes, such as the ones with the big Z on the vertical stabilizer, served with the 500th Bomb Group, 73rd Wing at Saipan. (MANN/SCHIRMER COLLECTION)

Totin To Tokyo was also moth-balled at Davis-Monathan AFB, one of the largest storage facilities in the United States. The Superfort completed 15 bombing missions against Japan before WWII ended, serving with the 58th Wing, 468th Bomb Group, 793rd Squadron at West Field, Tinian. This and the other photos of "mothballed" B-29s in this section were taken by Col. Schirmer, who was stationed at Davis-Monathan

AFB during the period the Superforts were stored there. (MANN/SCHIRMER COLLECTION)

Flak-Maid was a veteran of both the CBI Theatre and the Mariana Island Superfort assault against Japanese targets, flying from Indian bases and West Field on Tinian. The aircraft was with the 444th Bomb Group. By 1947, the *Maid* was a victim of the scrap heap, and her smooth-skinned aluminum fuselage and wings were destined to become pots and pans for lots of house-wives. (KEN RUST)

Jolly Roger, sporting a patch-eyed pirate, was a veteran of a two front Superfort effort against Japan. *Jolly* had experience doing it all. While stationed with the 468th Bomb Group, 58th BG

in India, the plane's crew flew four supply trips over the Himalayan Mountains, called the "Hump," as indicated by the four camel symbols, and ten regular bombing missions against Japanese targets. After moving to West Field on Tinian Island in the Pacific, the crew flew 18 missions to targets in the Japanese home islands. It was moth-balled at Davis-Monathan AFB, Tucson. (MANN / SCHIRMER COLLECTION)

THE KOREAN WAR IN COLOR

Final preparations for the next mission out of Kadena AB for this 372nd Bomb Squadron B-29. The flight crews have arrived and the ground crews are going over last-minute details. On November 8, 1950, a large formation of B-29s hit Sinuiju with incendiaries and the results were so effective that it was temporarily removed from the target list by Bomber Command. (CHARLES HIGGINS)

One of the rarest types of missions for the B-29 in the Korean War...a low-level daylight. This mission was flown by the 307th Bomb Group against supply routes in North Korea and, more than likely, the bomber formation had top cover of F-86s that could not be seen in this picture. Most of the MiG attacks against the B-29s were when they had no escort. At this low altitude, the aircraft would be very vulnerable to ground fire. (TED LONGMAN)

The only time that the ground crews got to rest was when their aircraft were airborne and en route or returning from a mission. If the Group was scheduled for a night mission, they worked all day and if it was a daylight raid, it meant working all night. A countless number of specialists swarmed all over the big bombers when they were on the ground. Most of the B-29s used in the Korean War had World War II time and were war weary, so it was the maintenance people that worked the miracles, as shown here on this 19th Group aircraft. (CHARLES BEARD)

A 19th Bomb Group Super-fortress gets a new prop at its base on Okinawa. This picture was taken in the late spring of 1953, when the bombers were flying night missions and receiving excellent protection from the Marine F3Ds. The Marine Night Fighters could mingle within the bomber stream, making it hard for the MiGs to figure out where they were. More than likely, the prop

change was due to fatigue and not damage from night flying MiG-15s. (LOUIS BRANCH)

Ground crews change out an engine on a 307th GroupB-29 at Kadena. Even though the experienced maintenance people did a great job, there was still the chance of a malfunction cropping up at a critical time right after take-off. Many of these resulted in disaster. It was standard procedure to have three SA-16s (Air-Sea Rescue)

spaced out over the entire bomber route to the target, just in case one of them had to ditch in the ocean en route or returning from the mission. (DAVID SYMES)

Ace in the Hole, a 98nd Bomb Group B-29, photographed at Kimpo AB (K-14), South Korea, with heavy battle damage. Kimpo and Taegu were emergency bases for the B-29s that had sustained too much damage to return to their main bases. Enough repairs were done at these bases to allow the aircraft to return to

Yokota AB or Kadena. The pilot of this B-29 was Lt. James Alexander. (C.E. ATKINSON)

A high altitude, daylight mission over North Korea by the 93rd Bomb Squadron, 19th Group. This mission was flown in June, 1951, when the Chinese had suffered heavy casualties and were in the process of retreating out of South Korea. Their massive "Fifth Phase" offensive had been a disaster. The medium bombers from Okinawa and Japan pounded the communist supply routes by day and the B-26s bombed them by night. (JAMES LYNCH)

A formation of 30th Bomb Squadron B-29s returning from a bomb mission over North Korea in 1951. The name of this aircraft was *Blue Tail Fly*. The squadron emblem was painted on all of the vertical stabilizers. The

30th's parent Group (19th) along with the 98th and 307th Groups were in combat over Korea for almost the entire length of the war. Two of SAC's Groups, the 22nd and 92nd went home in late October, 1950, before the Chinese entered the war. (BOB AMENDOLEA)

A mixture of two squadrons of the 19th Group flying a mission during the first winter of the war (December, 1950). Even though the MiG-15s had only been active for a few weeks, the low level, daylight mission was the most dangerous. From the appearance of the mountainous terrain, this mission was over the northern sectors of the Korean Peninsula. Note that none of the undersides of these B-29s had been painted black. This would change in early 1951. (ROBERT WOLLITZ)

A formation of B-29s from the 307th Bomb Group drop their loads over North Korea on a daylight mission in late 1950. On 23 January, 1951, the 19th and 307th Groups sent 21 B-29s to bomb Pyongyang's Main Airfield. Ninety-percent of their bombs hit squarely on the runway and put it out of operation for several days. Flak was light and all aircraft returned to Kadena. (GEORGE GRADEL)

A formation of B-29s from the 93rd Bomb Squadron en route to bomb Taejon on October 22, 1951. The Indian Head emblem of the 93rd can be seen painted on the tail. During the first six months of 1951, the Chinese troops and their supplies were devastated by the efforts of Bomber Command and the Air Force/Marine fighter bombers. Eighth Army HQ estimated that the Chinese lost 38,000 men during the first twenty-six days of January alone. (CHUCK BAISDEN)

A group of 307th officers gather out on the line during a down day. Many of the pictures taken at Kadena were done on just such occasions. This was during the fall of 1952. Note that the aircraft had a heavy coat of flat black paint on their undersides because the searchlights that were operating up along the Yalu River were extremely effective during the latter stages of the war. With the communist radar, based in Manchuria, controlling the AAA, it would have been fatal to be trapped in the lights. (FRANK SYLVESTER)

KOREAN WAR

A good close up view of the tail section of a 307th B-29 parked at Kadena in 1951. The aircraft could bring a heavy concentration of fire to anything trying to come up from the rear. The tail guns were manned and the bottom rear turret was part of a central fire control that was deadly accurate. (CHARLES HIGGINS)

Stateside Reject, a 19th Bomb Group B-29 parked on the ramp at Kadena in late summer of 1950. The upcoming mission requires the huge 1,000-pound G-P bombs as noted on the ground prior to loading. Early B-29 bomber operations in the Far East were set up by Major General Emmett O'Donnell. In Japan and for a brief period, it had five bomb groups and a Reconnaissance Squadron at its disposal. (W. J. BARTOL)

B-29s and 500-pound bombs for as far as the eye can see. In the background are 19th Bomb Group Superfortresses and in the foreground are the "Square Y" tails of the 307th Group. The 19th was the first Group in Korea to drop the massive 4,000-pound bombs against the bridges at Seoul on 13 August. They dropped 16 of them with limited results. It took four more days of bombing to drop the bridges. (BEN PARKISON)

A formation of 370th Bomb Squadron Superfortresses en route to their targets in North Korea. The missions were long and mostly over water. Even though they were only over the target area for minutes, it seemed much longer. In 1951, when this picture was taken, some days there were as many as 200 MiG-15s in the air waiting to

make a pass at the formations. The worst month for encountering enemy activity was the month of October, 1951. (BEN PARKISON)

At high altitude, during the day, the jagged mountain terrain of North Korea didn't look quite so ominous. These 372nd Bomb Squadron, 307th Bomb Group B-29s are preparing for a formation bomb drop. When the Panmunjon Peace Talks started in 1951, the MiGs became extremely aggressive against the B-29s. Once the bombers made landfall, they were in harm's way. (CHARLES HIGGINS)

Very rare shot of a KB-29M at Yokota Air Base, Japan in June, 1953. This was one of the first versions of the new B-29 tankers. The aircraft number was 44-87601 and it was assigned to Detachment-4 of the 98th Bomb Wing. Most of the refueling activities of these tankers were spent working with the F-84G models that had been pulled out of combat and moved to Japan to work on delivery of atomic weapons. (ROBERT MAIER)

KOREAN WAR

Not all of the stories to come out of Korea had a happy ending. This 307th B-29 suffered severe battle damage while on a bomb run over North Korea. The crippled bomber could not make it back to its base on Okinawa, so it diverted to Taegu Air Base for an emergency landing. In the approach, it hit the top of a hill and disintegrated. Wreckage was scattered over a wide area. (CHARLES HIGGINS)

A 19th Bomb Group B-29 touches down at Kadena AB in late summer of 1950. When the Pusan Perimeter looked like it was going to collapse, emergency orders were received by the 19th to download all heavy bombs and reload with 100-pound bombs. They were strung on thin wires and hung on bomb shackles in clusters of six. Each bomber carried about 20,000 pounds. Their mission was to hit the massing North Korean troops that were preparing to break through the perimeter. The attack wiped out a significant number of enemy troops and broke the back of the offensive. (CHARLES BEARD)

No Sweat from the 28th Bomb Squadron in perfect formation with other Superfortresses from the squadron, en route to North Korea. The 19th Bomb Group was comprised of three Bomb Squadrons; the 28th, 30th and 93rd. All three of these units did an outstanding job during the course of the war. The 19th had been heavily involved in combat in the Pacific. (ROBERT WOLLITZ)

B-29 PHOTO COMBAT DIARY

Late afternoon departure for the long flight to North Korea. A 19th Group bomber moves out toward the main runway at Kadena sometime in 1952. The symbol painted on the tail indicates that this aircraft was assigned to the 30th Bomb Squadron. During the course of the Korean War, the 19th Group lost several B-29s to operational mishaps. (FRANK SYLVESTER)

The fighter pilots were the favorites of the International Press because of the air-to-air combat. The reason for this is that the public was interested in it, so they wrote about it. Probably the most heralded B-29 to emerge from the Korean War was *Command Decision*. It had the distinction of being the only non-fighter type to shoot down five MiG-15s. Four of the gunner's visit with Colonel Breckenridge after they had made their fifth kill. On the far right is Corporal Harry Ruch who had a confirmed MiG-15 kill on October 27, 1951. (BERNARD STEIN)

On the 26th of July, 1950, FEAF had a total of eighty B-29s assigned in theatre. General MacArthur stated that if he could get seven missions per month out of each bomber, he would be happy. General O'Donnell said he would get far more than that out of them and that he intended to drop 5,500 tons of bombs per month. This would better the peak record of B-29 Ops from the Mariannas during World War II. *Mission Inn*

was one of the hard-working Superfortresses of the 22nd Bomb Group. (W. J. BARTOL)

No Sweat, a 19th Bomb Group B-29, is showing some wear and tear after many months of long missions and bad weather. On 23 March, 1951, forty-five F-86 Sabres tangled with a massive formation of MiGs above the Yalu River. The Sabres were top cover for twenty-two B-29s, from the 19th and 307th Groups, that slipped in and destroyed the rail bridges at Kogunyong and Chongju. (JOHN JOHNSON)

Battle damage received on a mission over the Yalu River caused this 307th Bomb Group B-29 to land at Pusan, South Korea for interim repairs. The conditions at this base on the southern tip of South Korea were still crude as the PSP can attest. A few months prior to this picture, the siege of the Pusan Perimeter had been going on and the weight of heavy transports bringing in supplies took its toll on the runways. (KEN LAMOREUX)

The damaged (307th Bomb Group) B-29 had been repaired enough for the flight back to Okinawa. This picture shows just how dangerous it could be in a heavily loaded aircraft taking off from Pusan, flying out over the harbor filled with ammunition ships. In the right corner of this picture is a B-26 from the 452nd Bomb Wing. (ROBERT HANSEN)

This B-29 has been modified to carry the huge 12,000-pound Tarzon bombs that were used against bridges. Note the difference in the size of the mission symbols and also the fact that this 19th Group Superfortress had shot down two MiG-15s. On 13 January, 1951, a lone B-29 dropped a Tarzon bomb on the railway bridge at Kanggye from 15,000

feet. The impact was so destructive that it dropped two spans into the water. (BERNARD STEIN)

A KB-29 refuels an F-84G over the Sea of Japan during the summer of 1953. This tanker was part of Detachment-4 of the 98th Bomb Group operating out Yokota AB, Japan. Note that the gun turrets have been removed. The KB-29 and KB-50 helped perfect the art of aerial refueling and when the KC-97 came

into operation, there was a solid core of trained people that were ready. (PAUL GIGUERE)

1st Lt. Louis Branch's crew makes final preparation for return to the United States after the Korean War. This was a 19th Bomb Group B-29 that had operated from Kadena Air Base on Okinawa. Needless to say that other, less fortunate, members of the 19th had a few things to say about the departure and the fact that this crew was getting to go back to the states. (LOUIS BRANCH)

On Okinawa during the summer of 1951, the only comfortable place was under the wing of a B-29 in the shade. A few of the B-29's aircrew await the ordnance people to show up and load their 307th Bomb Group Superfortress with 500-pound General Purpose bombs. To the flight crews, there was a marked difference between the lush green rolling landscape of Okinawa and the austere mountains of North Korea. (CHARLES HIGGINS)

A 307th Bomb Group B-29 fires up all four engines as it prepares to taxi out to the main runway for a daylight mission over North Korea. During the summer and fall of 1952, the 307th and 19th flew numerous sorties north of the front lines as the Chinese were attempting to mass their supplies and troops for an

offensive. FEAF Bomber Command was always responsive to any attempts by enemy troops to mount an offensive. (FRANK SYLVESTER)

Command Decision, a 19th Bomb Group Superfortress limps back to Kadena, with a feathered prop, after sustaining battle damage over North Korea. The holes in the wing appear to be from AAA as the MiG-15 was armed with cannon that could do much more extensive damage. This mission was in May, 1951. (BERNARD STEIN)

B-29 PHOTO COMBAT DIARY

The remains of a 98th Group B-29 that was not so fortunate. Badly damaged over its target, the pilot could not nurse it all the way to safety, but he did come close. The crash scene was less than two miles from the runway at Taegu AB. Details on survivors was not available. This was taken in the fall of 1950. (TOM GERZEL)

A 30th Bomb Squadron bombardier relaxes as his B-29 makes the long trek over water to North Korea. Three of the most dangerous targets assigned to the bombers were the key rail bridges at Kogunyong, Kwaksan and Chongju. These were well within the range of the MiG-15 and heavily defended with radar-controlled AAA. (LOUIS BRANCH)

The Korean War had been going on for about three months and it was still hot on Okinawa. Many of the B-29s were coming back with battle damage and one or more engines shot up. This 19th Bomb Group bomber is undergoing engine changes. Note the framework of a work cover that could be used in inclement weather or to protect the maintenance crews

from the hot sun. Most, if not all maintenance was done out in the open. (CHARLES BEARD)

From under the wing of a 307th Bomb Group bomber, a crewman snaps a picture of a neighboring 19th Group B-29 taxiing out for a daylight mission. In July, 1951, the daylight missions brought out the MiGs. On 9 July, several enemy jet fighters intercepted six 19th Group aircraft as they were turning off their bomb run against the Sinanju Airfield. Fortunately, the F-86 top cover got into the hassle and shot down one MiG while the Superfortress gunners destroyed another. (FRANK SYLVESTER)

Sucoshi Ni!, an RB-29 from the 91st Strategic Reconnaissance Squadron at Yokota AB, Japan in late 1951. Parked to the left of the RB is a KB-29 which was the tanker version of the B-29. Both of these units were attached to the 98th Bomb Group. Beginning in November 1951, the RB-29s were not allowed to fly missions into the MiG Alley area because they did not have the speed to deal with the enemy fighters. (DON SEESENGUTH)

KB-29M, Serial Number 44-27268 parked on the ramp at Yokota Air Base in early summer of 1953. This aircraft was the former B-29-35-NO, then serving as a tanker with Detachment-4 of the 98th Bomb Wing. This aircraft was part of "Project Fox" that refueled the F-84Gs of the 9th Fighter Bomber Squadron over Japan. (ROBERT MAIER)

B-29 PHOTO COMBAT DIARY

Head-on shot of a B-29 parked in its revetment on Kadena. Lined up in a neat row on the right are the "Y" tails of the 307th Bomb Group. On the far side of the field behind the B-29 are the Superforts of the 19th Bomb Group. These two Groups flew combat for most of the Korean War. They were also the only B-29 units that used Kadena after the 22nd Bomb Group left in the fall of 1950. (DAVID SYMES)

At altitude over their target, B-29s from the 93rd Bomb Squadron unload 500-pound G-P bombs in unison. In October, 1951, the Superforts suffered heavy losses. Due to intense MiG-15 attacks, five bombers were shot down and 55 crewmen were either killed in action or missing. Eight of the aircraft made it back to friendly bases with heavy damage. (BERNARD STEIN)

An unusual scene at Suwon...a big Superfortress. This 19th Group B-29 has probably set down for some mechanical reasons. There is no visible battle damage and at this late date in the war (1953), the F-86s controlled the skies over MiG Alley during the day and at night, the Marine F3Ds kept the enemy night fighters com-

pletely away from the bomber formations. (JACK TAYLOR)

KOREAN WAR

125

JITA meaning Jab In The Ass...a 19th Group B-29 is pictured here at Kadena in late 1950. The gunners on this aircraft had numerous gun battles with the MiGs in November and December of 1950. *JITA* was lost over North Korea in 1951. (JAMES STARK)

Rough Roman silhouettes a typical hot summer day at Kadena AB in August, 1950. This 19th Group Superfort along with several others flew a devastating mission against the military supply center at Kanggye on November 5th, 1950, in which 170 tons of incendiary bombs were dropped. The target was evaluated after the strike from photos taken by a

photo-recce aircraft and over 65% of the area had been burned out. (CHARLES BEARD)

A familiar and welcome sight to hundreds of B-29 aircrews that served in the Pacific from 1945 thru 1953. The final approach to Kadena Air Base on Okinawa. Most of the missions flown by the Superfortresses during the Korean War were from this base. At one time, there were three Bomb Groups operating here. (JIM LYNCH)

A damaged 98th Bomb Group Superfortress rests at Kimpo Air Base in the fall of 1952, while an F-86 Sabre from the 336th Fighter Interceptor Squadron taxies out. The F-86s kept the MiG-15s from getting to the bombers on most of the daylight missions over North

Korea. Some of the most exciting air battles that have been fought in the history of military aviation were fought between the Sabre and the MiG. (GROVER DOSTER)

During the early days at Kimpo Air Base 1950. This RB-29 was assigned to the 31st Strategic Reconnaissance Squadron, which would soon become the 91st Squadron. In the background Grumman F7F Tigercats flown by Marine Night Fighters VMF(N)542. The Marine fighters ran low level missions, at night against

trains and truck traffic. This mission was shared by the Douglas B-26 Invaders. (ED JOHNSON)

A 19th Group B-29 barely made it to a friendly airfield at Suwon, South Korea, in August, 1952, after it was jumped by a large formation of MiG-15s. Once on the ground, it was determined that there were over 100 holes in the airframe from the attack. The crew was lucky, because several

Superforts were shot down in the course of the war from far less hits than that. Even with F-86 protection, the MiGs were always numerically superior. (PHIL HUNT)

A graphic picture of just how close the B-29 crews were to disaster while on their bombing missions over North Korea during daylight hours. This 19th Bomb Group aircraft barely made it back to the closest base at Kimpo, South Korea during the early months of 1951. One prop is feathered and the engine was on fire when it landed. Quick response by the base fire fighters got the fire out and the Superfortress was flying missions a few days after this was taken. (GEORGE OLA)

Honeybucket Honshos, an elaborately painted RB-29 from the 91st Strategic Reconnaissance Squadron parked at Yokota AB, Japan sometime in 1951. The 91st replaced the 31st SRS on the 16th of November, 1950. These large recon aircraft had been providing FEAF Bomber Command with most of its target and bomb-damage assessment photography as far north as the Yalu River. In early

November, the RB-29s ran into a serious problem—the MiG-15. (David Mullen)

One of the most publicized B-29s to come out of the 19th Group...*The Outlaw*. This was named for the Jane Russell movie of the same name. This aircraft was flying with the 19th when they moved into Kadena AB during the first days of the war. This picture was taken in November, 1950. During the course of the war, only 16 Superfortresses were shot out of the sky by enemy fighters. The publicity that was given to this subject by the press would have the public believing that several were being shot down each week. (Robert Wollitz)

THE KOREAN WAR IN BLACK AND WHITE

The Boeing B-29 Superfortress was designed and produced with only one purpose in mind...to destroy the Japanese War Machine from the air and help bring an end to World War II. Its main competitors, during the final year of the war, were all older and outdated (the B-17 and B-24). When the war ended in 1945, the massive B-36 bomber was in the inventory and by the time the Korean War broke out in June, 1950, the Boeing B-47 was just about ready for mass production. The B-29 had become obsolete within a year after the end of World War II.

The war in Korea caught the U.S. government by surprise; its giant war machine had been dismantled, and the U.S. military presence in the Far East was pitiful. One of the first lessons learned was that the "all-jet" Air Force did not have the "legs" to fly from Japan, strike targets and return. The F-51 Mustang was rapidly brought into Japan from the states. There were two other World War II vintage warhorses that could be used quickly: the B-26 and the B-29.

The B-29 set an example that would be hard to match in this day and age of smart weapons, Mach 2 speeds and electronic warfare. A slow, World War II bomber, it held its own for almost the entire duration of the war. They flew long distances to their targets, waded through radar guided AAA, searchlights and last, but not least, had to defend them-

The "Square-Y" emblems painted on the tails of these B-29s meant that they were all assigned to the 307th Bomg Group operating off of Kadena AB on Okinawa. The crude conditions were reminiscent of World War II days in the Pacific. The 307th flew from McDill AFB, Florida to Kadena AB on 4 August, 1950, where they would operate until August, 1953. (WILLIAM GASKILL)

selves against the Soviet produced MiG-15 that were flown by experienced Russians pilots!

The Superfortresses put the key targets in North Korea out of business, in short order. Most of their assignments from the fall of 1950 until July, 1953, were in the extreme northern sectors of North Korea, also known as "Mig Alley." The aircrews were a mixture of the young and inexperienced combined with experienced veterans.

Although it was thought that a significant percentage of the B-29s were shot down, that just isn't the case. There were a total of 34 Superforts lost during the Korean War. Sixteen of these went down under the cannons of the MiG. Four were lost to AAA and fourteen were attributed to operational loss.

It was very costly for the MiGs to make a firing run on a formation of B-29s. With their fire control systems, numerous .50-caliber guns would form an accurate lead gauntlet for the MiG and sixteen of them were shot down along with seventeen other communist aircraft. There were countless numbers of MiGs that limped home, riddled with holes. On the other hand, there were a large number of B-29s that limped to nearby, friendly bases with battle damage.

The B-29 did an absolutely magnificent job in the Korean War. The key to this record lies with both the ground and air crews. They were skilled, experienced and motivated. And, even today, those three ingredients are the key to success for any Fighter or Bomb Wing.

FUJIGMO, a 19th Bomb Group aircraft is prepared for another mission over Korea in late 1950. The 19th operated from Kadena AB, Okinawa for the entire time it was committed to the war. The name on the aircraft was a popular phrase, at the time, meaning "F___ You Joe, I've Got My Orders". This base had been one of the main operational bases in the Pacific, since its capture from the Japanese in 1945. Today, it is one of the most modern air bases in the world. (RICHARD OAKLEY)

Ground crews prepare one of the 19th Bomb Group B-29s for another night mission over North Korea. The Bomb Group's emblem is painted on the left side of the cockpit on this bomber. Note the black camouflage paint scheme on the bottom of the aircraft. This proved to be very effective in preventing the search lights from picking them up at night. (RICHARD OAKLEY)

An unidentified pilot and the crew chief on this RB-29 discuss potential problems after a long recon mission over the extreme northern sectors of North Korea. The 91st Strategic Reconnaissance Squadron was attached to the Far East Air Forces during the Korean War and operated out of Yokota Air Base, Japan. The 91st had a long and colorful history dating back to 1917, when it was designated the 91st Aero Squadron. (W.J. BARTOL)

Crew members of a 33rd Bomb Squadron B-29 pose beside their aircraft on Kadena in September, 1950. The 22nd Bomb Group was based at March AFB, California, when the Korean War broke out. They were immediately alerted for combat and moved to Okinawa. Note the 22nd Bomb Group emblem on the side of the bomber. On the extreme left is the pilot; Captain Fred Farrell and next to him is the co-pilot, 2nd Lt. Ken Plumeau. (KEN PLUMEAU)

The entire 30th Bomb Squadron of the 19th Bomb Group gather on and in front of one of their B-29s at Kadena, for a squadron picture. This demonstrates just how enormous the big Boeing bomber was. At the start of the Korean War, FEAF had only 22 operational B-29s. (FRED TRIPPEL)

This 19th Bomb Group B-29 was one that had dropped the precision 1,000 pound Razon Bombs. The bombs had remotely controlled tail fins that could be controlled by the bombardier's radio signals. These were probably the first "smart" bombs and it met with limited success during the early going. By the time that the final 150 of these bombs were dropped, they showed remarkable results against bridges. (RICHARD OAKLEY)

It is early morning on Okinawa and the ground crews have converged on the big bombers that had flown on missions the night before. Everything has to be checked and rechecked on these 307th B-29s before they are loaded with bombs for the next night mission over the extreme northern sector of North Korea. The black paint scheme is to protect against the glaring searchlights. (C.E. JORDAN)

B-29 PHOTO COMBAT DIARY

A 30th Bomb Squadron B-29 lets go with a full load of 500-pound G-P bombs out of both bomb bays, over North Korea. The high altitude daylight missions proved to be very costly as the slow bombers were vulnerable to the accurate AAA and the MiG-15s that were operating out of bases in Manchuria. (FRED TRIPPEL)

Rows of 500-pound General Purpose bombs line the edge of the hardstands on Kadena as B-29 ground crews await the arrival of the bomb loading crews. This area of the base was assigned to the 307th Bomb Group which would fly combat missions against North Korea until the end of the war. (C.E. JORDAN)

One of the most combat experienced B-29s flying from Okinawa in 1952. This bomber had flown 115 missions over North Korea with the 307th Bomb Group. On the large bomb emblem painted on the side is the number "100" with an additional 15 small bomb symbols showing next to the pilot's position. Sgt. Chiddix, one of the gunners, is shown standing next to the lower gun turret. (WILLIAM GASKILL)

KOREAN WAR

Four members of a B-29 flight crew wait as their aircraft receives final preparations for another night mission over North Korea. These 19th Bomb Group members logged hundreds of hours in the air on the long flights to the target. During the first few weeks of the war, the 19th was used to bomb small towns close to the 38th parallel in an attempt to slow down the push to the south by the North Korean ground forces. (RICHARD ALLEN)

The 28th Bomb Squadron sign in front of their operations center on Kadena in 1951. The 28th was one of the oldest in the Air Force, with its beginning in 1917. It was not until during World War II that the 28th became part of the 19th Bomb Group. They flew the B-29 from 1944 until 1954. (RICHARD OAKLEY)

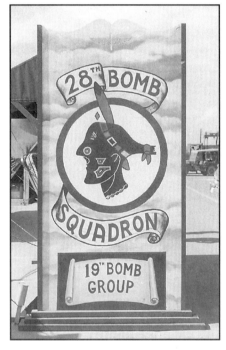

Lucky Dog, a B-29 assigned to the 19th Bomb Group undergoing engine changes on the port side. With the experience level of the maintenance crews, engine changes and other major maintenance were handled quickly. Since the aircraft were all parked out in the open, it was fortunate that the weather on Okinawa was rather good. (RICHARD FRYER)

B-29 PHOTO COMBAT DIARY

One of the most dramatic pictures taken during the Korean War shows a 98th Bomb Group B-29 making a low level daylight bomb run over a North Korean airfield. The bomber and its shadow can be seen in close proximity. The picture was taken by a 91st Strategic Reconnaissance Squadron RB-29 from a higher altitude. (VERN VAN NOPPEN)

A seasoned veteran heading north again. The Circle "X" on the tail designates this as an RB-29 assigned to the 91st Strategic Recon Squadron out of Yokota AB, Japan. Note the numerous mission symbols painted on the left side of the nose. This picture was taken in 1951 as the aircraft was heading out for a mission over North Korea. (VERN VAN NOPPEN)

Some of the aircrew for this 19th Group B-29 pose in front of their bomber shortly before they are to take off from Kadena AB, Okinawa on a bomb mission over North Korea. The 19th was used during the first days of the war, to run the rails leading south in an effort to disrupt enemy rail traffic. This tactic was not effective at all. (RICHARD ALLEN)

The B-29s did everything they could to give the North Korean industrial complex the "Purple Shaft." This 19th Bomb Group bomber is parked on its hardstand at Kadena AB in the summer of 1951. During the famous Inchon Invasion, the heavy bombers were directed to hit all roads and rail lines leading into the Seoul area. This would stop any attempt to reinforce the enemy troops at the landing site. (RICHARD OAKLEY)

The sign that was displayed in front of the 19th Bomb Group's Headquarters on Okinawa. As you can readily see, the Group had some strong blood lines dating back to 1927. Their history had been written in the Pacific. They were the first B-29 outfit to bomb Korea, when on the 28th of June, 1950, they were ordered to strike targets of opportunity north of Seoul, such as assembly points for tanks and troops. (RICHARD ALLEN)

Superfortresses from the 92nd Bomb Group bear down on a daylight bomb run along the south side of the Yalu River. Note the bursts of flak above the formation. The 92nd, along with the 22nd Group, flew missions against North Korean targets until they were pulled out of combat in October, 1950. The 92nd would soon convert over to the new super Bomber B-36. (JOE KONCHALSKI)

Keeping the B-29's .50-caliber machine guns cleaned and in perfect working order was essential to the survival of the bomber and its crew. On numerous occasions, the rendezvous between the bomber stream and the top cover fighters did not happen and the B-29s continued on to their targets. The enemy radar would pick up on this and the MiG-15s would swarm all over the formations. The concentrated fire of the .50-caliber guns made it extremely difficult for the communist jets and though many B-29s were shot down, there were numerous casualties among the enemy ranks. (RICHARD OAKLEY)

Ground crews of the 22nd Bomb Group repair battle damage on one of the big Superfort's engines. The bomb trucks have not arrived yet with another massive load of 500-pound G-P's for the upcoming mission. This picture was taken in late summer of 1950, about the time that the Inchon Invasion took place. Every B-29 that could fly was involved in this mission. Supplies and reinforcements to the out-flanked North Korean Army were virtually cut-off because of the efforts of the bombers and fighter bombers. (HAL STRACK)

Major George Ham's crew pose by one of the most colorful B-29s in the 22nd Bomb Group. These crews were some of the most experienced in SAC, with most having World War II time.

On the 28th of July, 1950, the 22nd was ordered to hit the rail marshalling yards at Seoul again. Enemy air activity had been heavy in the area, so the gunners were prepared for anything. At this time, the North Korean Yaks were trying their luck against the big bombers, but with a deadly central fire control on board the B-29s, the Yaks took a beating if they got close enough. (HAL STRACK)

Late afternoon on Okinawa and this 30th Bomb Squadron B-29 is receiving final preparations for the evening's mission. With the war only six weeks old, FEAF planners figured they could destroy the entire industrial complex of North Korea, using every available B-29 in the theatre. The weapon of choice

would be incendiary bombs, but this plan was scrapped due to the possibility of high casualties among civilians in the large cities like Pyongyang. (RICHARD ALLEN)

Sgt. John Chernyk, a flight engineer in the 19th Bomb Squadron / 22nd Bomb Group stands in front of B-29 #529 while it goes through a run-up on one of its starboard engines. This picture was taken in late summer of 1950. The 22nd moved 8,000 miles to Okinawa and flew its first combat mission on 13 July, 1950, only nine days after receiving orders. This was an example of how mobile the

Strategic Air Command had become in the short time of its existence. (HAL STRACK)

The bomb trucks have just finished piling the bombs in one of the B-29 revetments for the night's mission. It is hard to imagine the tonnage that a group of B-29s could drop on a target. Keep in mind, that by the end of 1950, the number of quality targets left in North Korea were very few. The 19th Bomb Group, alone, flew 622 combat missions during the Korean War and dropped 49,000 tons of

bombs, most of which was concentrated in the upper reaches of North Korea where the MiG-15s and AAA were the deadliest. (RICHARD ALLEN)

KOREAN WAR

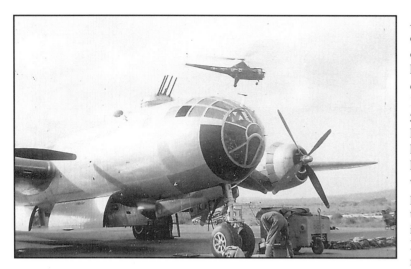

As an Air-Sea Rescue helicopter moves overhead in the background, an aircrew member of this 19th Bomb Group B-29 prepares to put his personal gear on board. In late October, 1950, the Group was temporarily pulled out of combat to update the training of its crews. However, the Chinese entered the war in early November, and the 19th was rushed back into combat on the 6th of November to bomb the bridges that spanned the Yalu River. (PAUL MOON)

The B-29 that usually bedded down in this revetment is out on a mission, but details are already being handled for the following day's mission. The bomb trucks have made their haul from the bomb dump and the bombs to be used on the next mission have been placed in their proper place awaiting the loading crew. They will attach the fins on the bombs prior to loading them in the bomber. This scene is on the 19th Group ramp at Kadena AB. (RICHARD ALLEN)

South Sea Sinner, a 19th Bomb Group aircraft parked at Kadena AB. During the early days of the Korean War, there were three B-29 Groups in theatre. Two of these were used for inter-diction and the other would temporarily be used for close support. The quick buildup of fighter bomber aircraft in Japan and South Korea allowed the big bombers to go after strategic targets up along the Yalu River. (RICHARD OAKLEY)

A significant photograph taken on 12 March, 1952. This bomb represented the 30,000th ton of bombs that the 307th Bomb Group had dropped over targets in North Korea since their entry into the war. Left to right; Lt. Jack Bush; aircraft commander, Lt. Wes Hills; bombardier and Karl Kristofferson, central fire control. This was taken at the group's base at Kadena right before the ordnance crews loaded the aircraft. (KARL KRISTOFFERSON)

The bombardier on a 19th Group B-29 gets a first rate view of the scenery and the upcoming target. The aircraft commander and the co-pilot stations are immediately behind the bombardier. The visibility from the front of the Boeing bomber was excellent. When the war broke out, the 19th had 23 operational B-29s assigned and with the war less than a week old, the Group had 21 of its aircraft ready to operate from Kadena Air Base on Okinawa. This was a remarkable accomplishment even by today's standards. (RICHARD ALLEN)

Aircraft Commander 1st Lt. Richard Allen (right) fills out all the forms for the debriefing of his crew after a long mission to North Korea from Kadena. Allen states that one of the toughest targets to go after was the Oriental Light Metal Works at Sinuiju. This target probably had the greatest concentration of searchlights around it and for a B-29 to go in at night without its bottom painted black, would invite a very rough bomb run. (RICHARD ALLEN)

KOREAN WAR

Loose formation over the Pacific en route to North Korea by 22nd Bomb Group B-29s. The tail code is clear in this shot, which identifies the Group. This was taken right after the 22nd reached their combat base at Kadena and no nose art had been painted on this aircraft. This unit was under the command of the Strategic Air Command. (HAL STRACK)

A talented artist works on one of his masterpieces, *Peace Maker*. Most of the nose art on the B-29s were painted on as the aircraft were being serviced between missions. The Circle "E" painted on the tails of these bombers indicated that they were assigned to the 22nd Bomb Group. The 22nd was one of the early Groups brought in from the states. They had compiled an impressive record in the Pacific during World War II, while flying the B-24s. (HAL STRACK)

Ace in the Hole shown here after all of the vital areas had been covered was assigned to the 98th Bomb Group out of Yokota Air Base, Japan. 2nd Lt. James Alexander was flying the right seat. During the fall of 1950, there were five Bomb Groups operating in the Far East, three were out of Kadena and two out of Yokota. This put a tremendous strain on both airfields and their facilities. (J.S. EDMONDSON)

The Aircraft Commander of this B-29 gets down to serious business prior to departure for a mission out of Kadena. The crew has all of their gear ready to be stowed on the bomber. The emblem painted on the side shows that it is from the 19th Bomb Group. During its production years, there were 3,970 B-29s built. A large percentage of the surviving fleet at the end of World War II were cocooned for future use. (RICHARD ALLEN)

Ground level view from the rear of a 307th aircraft. It is still several hours before take off time and all of the ground crew personnel are making sure that every write up is checked out and all maintenance is completed on time. Note the bomb truck has just arrived on the right side to deposit the load of bombs to be used on the night's mission. (CHARLES HIGGINS)

Armorers remove tracer rounds from the ammo belts in preparation for the upcoming night mission. Note the mission symbols for World War II and also Korea. This 307th B-29 had already accumulated 65 missions over North Korea, combined with 40 missions over Japan in World War II. This picture was taken in 1951 and the Group still had almost two years left in combat, so this aircraft, if it stayed in one piece, probably had one of the high times in combat. (CHARLES HIGGINS)

Another great paint job on a 98th Bomb Group B-29. *Mais Oui* was piloted by 1st Lt. Rob Tuttle out of Yokota Air Base, Japan. The 98th was ordered into the Korean War out of its home base at Fairchild AFB in July, 1950. They shared the Yokota base with the 91st Strategic Reconnaissance Squadron who were flying the RB-29. (J.S. EDMONDSON)

Four-a-Breast, a 19th Group B-29 parked in its revetment at Kadena during the spring of 1951. The B-29 in the distant background is from the 307th Group. At one time, in early fall of 1950, the sprawling base at Kadena was jammed with three Bomb Groups. With five Bomb Groups working under FEAF, there were 18 major strategic targets assigned to them during the August / September, 1950 period. By the 25th of September, all 18 had been destroyed. (RICHARD OAKLEY)

Battle damage from the night before on this 307th bomber called for an engine change which is being done the next day. It is amazing to imagine just how many man hours went into maintaining one of the B-29s, and in many cases, the Bomb Groups used the aircraft constantly for close to three years. Replacements were coming out of the storage facility stateside, but if it was humanly possible, the ground crews kept the ones they had in the air. (CHARLES HIGGINS)

B-29 PHOTO COMBAT DIARY

Night mission after bomb drop and away from the target area was time to relax a little. Here, the bombardier, Wes Hills, looks back for a picture as his B-29 makes the flight back to the 307th's base at Kadena. Night missions were slightly safer, but they still had to contend with radar controlled AAA and night flying MiG-15s. The guardian angels of the bombers, at night, were the F-94s and Marine F3Ds. (KARL KRISTOFFERSON)

A 22nd Bomb Group crew lines up for inspection prior to a mission. Fourth from the left shows Captain David C. Jones talking with the aircraft commander Major Hal Strack. Jones would continue on to achieve the rank of four-star General in the U.S. Air Force. All of the B-29 Groups were in place and going full bore in August 1950. They flew massive strikes against such targets as the Cho-Sen Nitrogen Explosives plant at Konan and the big Bogun Chemical Plant. (HAL STRACK)

Most of the pictures taken during wartime were snapped by crewmen as they were working on the line or preparing to fly a mission. On rare occasions, some of the crews were caught with full uniforms on and looking like they were ready for a formal inspection. This Photo Reconnaissance crew from the 91st Squadron poses in their dress blues. The aircraft commander is Captain Don Seesenguth. Note the lack of mission symbols on the side of the RB-29, so this could have been taken right after the crew arrived at Yokota, or the aircraft is a replacement that is new to the theatre. (DON SEESENGUTH)

1st Lt. Joe Robertson's *Haulin Ass* parked at Yokota Air Base. This aircraft was assigned to the 343rd Bomb Squadron of the 98th Bomb Group. This squadron did not start flying the B-29 until 1947. One year after the Korean War ended, they transitioned into SAC's new state-of-the-art B-47. The squadron lineage began in the bleak days of World War II (1942) and they would fly the B-24s in North Africa and Italy. (J.S. Edmondson)

A 91st Strategic Reconnaissance Squadron RB-29 appropriately named *Over Exposed*. During World War II, the 91st flew a couple of rare recon aircraft types; the F-10 (B-25) and the F-9 (B-17). During World War I, they flew the DH-4 and SPAD XIII out of numerous bases in France and Germany. (Don Seesenguth)

Lemon Drop Kid, a 19th Bomb Group B-29, showing a caricature of Bob Hope on its nose. Hope was the most popular entertainer that went over to Korea to help bring home to the servicemen. His efforts will never be forgotten by anyone that was in World War II, Korea or Vietnam. The green trim on the nose signifies that this aircraft was 28th Bomb Squadron, based at Kadena. (Paul Moon)

A very familiar B-29 to the International Press Corps. *Command Decision* was still going strong long after its original crew had rotated back to the states. Showing 64 missions and its "Ace" status MiG symbols, the new Aircraft Commander of the bomber was Captain Sam Wareham. (MARION BERRY)

A 307th Bomb Group B-29 salvoes its load of 1,000 pound bombs on a North Korean target from high altitude. This picture was taken from the right rear blister of another B-29 in the formation. During the early months of 1952, the 307th participated in some saturation bombing of all known North Korean airfields in an effort to make sure that they remained inoperable. All of these missions used 1,000 pound or larger bombs to produce the huge craters on the runways. (KARL KRISTOFFERSON)

Miss Jackie the Rebel, a 30th Bomb Squadron B-29 gets its windscreen polished by the crew chief. This squadron began its history as the 30th Aero Squadron on 13 June, 1917, and served in France during World War I. Its World War II heritage saw duty in Australia and ended up on North Field, Guam. When the B-29 was retired, they flew the B-47 and later the B-52. (KARL KRISTOFFERSON)

An unusual view of a B-29 on a high altitude mission to North Korea. The massive vertical stabilizer is clearly shown. In the spring of 1953, when all indications pointed to the war ending in a matter of weeks, the emphasis of bomber command shifted from the industrial targets back to airfields and bridges. The terms of the truce provided for a 12 hour free period between the time it was signed until it went into effect. This would give the communists a chance to bring in aircraft and equipment. Due to the heavy attacks by UN bombers and fighter bombers, the enemy was not given the chance to build up. (DEAN KELLER)

A very unusual photograph taken out of the bomb bay as a 22nd Bomb Group B-29 drops its load of 1000-pound bombs on a network of bridges in North Korea. The Yalu River can be seen below. This was taken in the early fall of 1950, before the Chinese entered the war. (BILL KAHLER)

Returning from a mission, this 307th Bomb Group Superfortress touches down at Kadena AB in early 1951. The B-29 probably received as much publicity as any aircraft type during the 1940s and early 1950s. The last one in USAF inventory was phased out of operation at 2010 hours on June 21, 1960. (PAUL MOON)

A newly arrived B-29 from the 22nd Bomb Group shows only five missions under its belt. The 22nd and 92nd Groups were initially under the control of SAC's 15th Air Force, but they were turned over to FEAF Bomber Command while they were involved in operations over Korea. During the early, chaotic days of the Korean War, the B-29s were used in visual attacks against ground support targets, which was a waste of the Superfortress's capability. (BILL KAHLER)

All the ingredients for conducting a successful bomb campaign are in this picture...B-29 with guns loaded and ready, aircrew arriving on the line with their gear, bombs stacked nearby for the next mission, and control tower ready to coordinate heavy outbound traffic. This aircraft is from the 19th Bomb Group and as this picture was taken not long after the Group arrived at Kadena, as there are not too many mission symbols showing...yet. (RICHARD ALLEN)

KOREAN WAR

149

When the 19th Group first got to Kadena, they were under control of 20th Air Force until July 8, 1950, when FEAF Bomber Command began operation. The Group's first loss in combat happened on July 12, 1950, when a formation of B-29s was attacked by enemy aircraft. A 28th Bomb Squadron bomber went down, with the crew bailing out. Nine of the crew were rescued, while two members were listed as missing in action. *Peace Maker* was assigned to the 19th Group. (RICHARD ALLEN)

Hot to Go, a 98th Bomb Group B-29 undergoes routine maintenance at Yokota prior to flying another mission. The pilot of this Superfort was 1st Lt. James Alexander. This was a replacement aircraft for his original *Ace in the Hole*. A short time after this picture was taken, the nose art was completely removed. (JAMES ALEXANDER)

If it were not for the beautiful female form and the cartoon characters, the war would have taken on a completely different image, as far as aircraft were concerned. *Bugs Buster* was a classic. In the background is *Blue Tail Fly*. Both of these Superfortresses were assigned to the 30th Bomb Squadron of the 19th Bomb Group. (RICHARD OAKLEY)

B-29 PHOTO COMBAT DIARY

A gunner looking out of the blister on the left side of his bomber observes another B-29 in formation while en route to their target. The mountains of North Korea can be seen in the lower part of the blister. The apparatus shown in this picture was an aiming and firing device that controlled several of the guns. It could put a heavy concentration of firepower on an incoming MiG-15. (PAUL MOON)

Rock Happy, a 19th Group aircraft, basks in the sun at Kadena, evidently waiting for a night mission. By November, 1950, the number of targets were diminishing significantly. Most of the B-29 missions had to be in the extreme northern parts of North Korea which was hazardous. During one daylight incendiary attack on the Hoeryong supply center, a large number of MiG-15s were sighted flying parallel to the bomber formation, but they made no effort to engage. (RICHARD OAKLEY)

During the first few months of the war, the B-29s had very little opposition in that the enemy had not yet set up heavy AAA around key targets and the MiG's had not appeared. The typical tactic for bridge busting was that the bombers would form a stream at about 10,000 feet and fly toward the bridge at a 40-degree angle to its span. Each B-29 triggered off four bombs on a single run. Statistics showed that in some cases, it took thirteen runs to destroy some of the bridges. *Miss Megook* was a 19th Bomb Group aircraft. (RICHARD OAKLEY)

One of the 19th Bomb Group's heavy haulers waits for the bomb loading crews to arrive. *Raz 'N Hell* was one of the first bombers to be rigged to carry the 1,000-pound Razon bombs that were guided to their target by radio signals transmitted by the bombardier. The fins were movable and responded to the signals. They did not always function as they were supposed to. Out of 489 Razon bombs dropped, 331 of them actually worked. (PAUL MOON)

Koza Kid waits for the bomb crews to load. This was a 19th Bomb Group B-29 based on Okinawa. This Group had the longest tenure in the Korean War, of the B-29 units. Its crews flew nearly 53,000 hours while flying 5,499 sorties. On the 29th of March, 1951, tragedy struck when one of its bombers went down in the East China Sea while it was en route to bomb Hamhung, with the Tarzon bomb on board. All of the crew was lost, including Colonel Payne Jennings, the 19th Group commander. (JAMES STARK)

The B-29 was involved in most of the 37 months of combat that encompassed the Korean War. During that period, very few, if any, of the aircraft escaped the artist's brush. Replacement bombers came in clean and when the war ended, those aircraft that were flying back to the states had their nose art painted over. But, no one will disagree that it was the art that gave each Superfortress its own identity and personality. *Miss N. C.* was assigned to the 19th Bomb Group. (KARL KRISTOFFERSON)

Staff Sgt. Royal A. Veatch, a gunner on this Tarzon bombing Superfortress, points to the MiG-15 "kills" his aircraft has made. Veatch was officially credited with shooting down one of the MiGs on April 12, 1951. This B-29 was flown by the 30th Bomb Squadron of the 19th Group out of Kadena. The symbols of the Tarzon missions were much larger than those of the regular missions. (ROYAL VEATCH)

Captain David Jones, a B-29 pilot from the 22nd Bomb Group, en route to a target in North Korea, during the fall of 1950. Jones would continue his career in the Air Force to the highest level. He achieved the rank of General (4 Stars) and became the Chief of Staff of the USAF along with Chairman of the Joint Chiefs of Staff. (HAL STRACK)

Left to right: Captains Smitherman and Matthew J. Hegerle are being congratulated by an officer from Group for their successful Tarzon Bomb drop on the bridge at Kanggye, North Korea on February 11, 1951. Two spans were dropped into the water. Their aircraft *Dead Jug* was from the 19th Bomb Group. (MATTHEW HEGERLE)

Late summer 1950 and plenty of heat and humidity to go around...*Southern Comfort* of the 19th Bomb Group is undergoing the usual ritual from its ground crew for the next mission. When World War II ended, there were still orders out for an additional 5,092 B-29s to be built. Following VJ Day, these orders were cancelled. (RICHARD OAKLEY)

The 98th Bomb Group got its orders to move to Japan, when the Strategic Air Command alerted the Group to proceed to Japan on 1 August, 1950. At the time, there were already three Bomb Groups flying combat missions, but very few of them had been against strategic targets. The 98th and 307th went over at the same time. *Sic 'Em* was a 98th aircraft operating out of Yokota Air base in Japan. (J.S. EDMONDSON)

Undergoing a prop change at Kadena, this B-29 probably had sustained battle damage to one of the blades and it would not take much of a hole or "nick" to cause serious problems. This 19th Bomb Group Superfortress was getting near the end of its combat tour as this was taken in July of 1953. (LOUIS BRANCH)

A pair of 307th Bomb Group B-29s return from a daylight mission in loose formation. Their final destination would be Kadena AB and home. Note the dark painted (antiglare) underside of the bomber. In 1951, most of B-29 missions had to be flown at night due to heavy damage

from accurate ground fire. The enemy searchlights were very accurate and this scheme made it very difficult for them to lock on. (MORRIS BORENE)

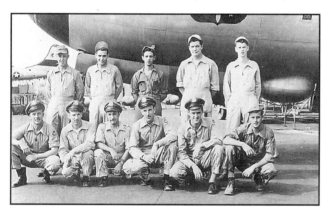

The original crew of *FUJIGMO* pose beside their bomber. According to Tail Gunner Sgt. Robert Schulenberg (top row, far right), "On 28 June, 1950, we were sent to bomb targets of opportunity near Seoul, South Korea. We bombed and strafed marshalling yards, tanks and troops concentrations near Uijongbu and at times we flew as low as 200 feet on strafing runs." (ROBERT SCHULENBERG)

Left to right: S/Sgt. Robert Spenard and Cpl. Harry Ruch take a look at damage done to their B-29, *Command Decision*, by a MiG-15. The mission was flown on 27 October, 1951, by the 28th Bomb Squadron. Cpl. Ruch was officially credited with shooting down a MiG on this same mission. This widely publicized bomber went on to achieve "Ace" status by shooting down five MiGs. (HARRY RUCH)

KOREAN WAR

155

Close formation of 307th Bomb Group aircraft over North Korea. The Block "Y" on the vertical stabilizer identifies the Group. The standard procedure for bombing rail marshalling yards was a four ship formation. Usually long and narrow, the yards could be covered from one end to the other with outstanding results. The ordnance for this mission was usually 500-pound general purpose bombs. (CHARLES HIGGINS)

Atomic Tom was one of the first B-29s from the 19th Bomb Group to fly a combat sortie against the advancing North Korean Army. They dropped their bombs south of the 38th Parallel. The priorities for the bombers during the first few days of the war were centered around road and rail traffic followed by going after the large bridges above Seoul. (JAMES LYNCH)

Butterfly Baby and her crew pose at Yokota Air Base in 1951. Standing at left is aircraft commander Captain Molloy and to his left is the pilot; 1st Lt. Vern van Noppen. The 91st Strategic Reconnaissance Squadron RB-29s usually had nose art on the right side and the squadron emblem painted on the left side. The 91st carried out a wide variety of missions to the north and many had nothing to do with the war in Korea, which meant they were monitoring China and the Soviet Union. (VERN VAN NOPPEN)

B-29 PHOTO COMBAT DIARY

The time is late July, 1953, the Korean War had just ended and this B-29 from the 19th Bomb Group is making final preparations to return back to the states. Note that the nose art had been painted over. (LOUIS BRANCH)

As far as this beautiful scene is concerned, the war was one million miles away. Sunset on Okinawa over the flightline of 28th Bomb Squadron Superfortresses. To observe this peaceful setting, it is hard to imagine that a few hours later, this bomber could be over North Korea, taking heavy flak and dodging the Soviet MiGs. (CHARLES BEARD)

A single 98th Bomb Group B-29 prepares to take off from Taegu Air Base after landing with battle damage. The code for this base was K-2 and it was a major base for the F-80s and F-84s during 1951. Though conditions remained primitive until late 1952, it was a safe-haven for countless B-29s that were shot up by AAA or the MiGs. The Superfortress shown here was en route back to its base at Yokota. (NAT KING)

KOREAN WAR

Captain Vance's crew line up by their *Sad Sac* before they were to fly a mission. During the 22nd Bomb Group's early days on Okinawa, they were teamed up with the 19th Group on a mission in which forty-seven B-29s hit the Seoul railway marshalling yards. This was on 13 July, 1950. They destroyed heavy tonnage of North Korean supplies meant for their advancing troops. (HAL STRACK)

One of the first B-29s to see action in the Korean War was BUB which stood for *Beat Up Bastard*. For the entire length of the Korean War (37 months), the B-29s flew missions on all but 26 days. When you consider that their aircraft were all World War II veterans, the enemy fighters, accurate AAA, and lousy weather, this was a remarkable record! (W. J. BARTOL)

Koza Kid parked under a beautiful sky. This 19th Group B-29 was named for a nearby village

on Okinawa. The tremendous toll extracted from the enemy in the way of casualties and loss of valuable supplies prompted the Chinese to bring in large concentrations of AAA guns and the effects of this among United Nations aircraft, including the B-29s, began to be felt in fall of 1951. (RICHARD ALLEN)

Aircraft Commander 1st Lt. Richard Allen poses by his bomber at Kadena. This aircraft was one of the top timers as one can determine from the mission symbols painted on the nose. Allen and his crew were one of the first to fly a combat mission over Korea. The blue nose color indicates that it is a 30th

Bomb Squadron bomber. For two weeks, the 19th was the only B-29 outfit in theatre and they logged 151 sorties during this brief period. (RICHARD ALLEN)

Sgt. James Stark,(far right), crew chief on *BUB*, poses with other members of the ground crew as they prepare their 19th Bomb Group aircraft for the upcoming night's mission. Note the clusters of small bombs that will be used against enemy troop concentrations and other similar targets. The Aircraft Commander on this bomber was Captain Bartol. *BUB* stood for *Beat Up Bastard*. (JIM STARK)

Captain Don Seesenguth, aircraft commander of this RB-29 briefs his crew on the upcoming mission out of Yokota AB, Japan. The 91st Strategic Reconnaissance Squadron flew many mission types other than over North Korea. They spent a lot of time off the coast of the Soviet Union around Port Arthur. Note the numerous photo mission symbols painted on the aircraft. (DON SEESENGUTH)

The Spirit of Freeport attracts the attention of Bob Hope and Marilyn Maxwell while they were visiting the 22nd Bomb Group's facilities on Kadena. This shot was taken in October of 1950, just before the 22nd was pulled out of combat and returned to their base in the states. (FRED TRIPPEL)

A few officers from the 22nd Bomb Group gather around two visiting entertainers; Bob Hope and Marilyn Maxwell. They provided countless shows for tens of thousands of servicemen involved in the Korean War. (FRED TRIPPEL)

Armament specialists work on the forward top turret on this 19th Group B-29, *Dragon Lady*. Several of the big bombers carried elaborate nose art and this was one of the best. The 19th was one of the first units to participate in the Korean War. On 25 June, 1950, they were stationed at North Field, Guam and were immediately ordered to move to Okinawa. (RICHARD OAKLEY)

B-29 PHOTO COMBAT DIARY